THE GATE

ETERNITY BECKONS

SCOTT R. SULLIVAN

Scott Sullivan
"Bringing the invisible world to life."

Table of Contents

PROLOGUE

This book is dedicated to all the people that feel
lonely, isolated, rejected, voiceless, and unseen.

You are heard, you are seen, and I hope this book
points you to the One Who has known you from the
very beginning.

INTRODUCTION

Desperation and need can be powerful forces in our lives. I have always found God the deepest when I have had the greatest need or I've been in the most desperate place. If our hearts desires are unbridled, then our own desperation can lead us to decisions that can bring hurt and pain upon ourselves and others. Desperation bridled with Wisdom, though, can open Heaven's opportunities over our lives and change the course of Eternity.

We live in a time in which so many people find their value and self-worth in career, social media, latest trends, fads, sports, talents, music, or material possessions. Not one of those categories is inherently wrong, but if our hearts' filters are not aligned correctly they can be very destructive. We all need to put our eyes Heavenward and find out where our true identity should be based. You have a destiny, a specific design, and you were created for a purpose. I hope this book brings you encouragement, hope, and a fiery drive to discover your destiny.

Heaven is an amazing place! My desire is to give you a glimpse of what awaits all of those who know Jesus. You can access much of Heaven now on earth and begin to walk out all of who you were created to be.

Thank you for purchasing this book! Please jump over to my Facebook page (search for "Scott R Sullivan Author") where there is a community of people walking this journey with you. I also have a YouTube channel (search for "Scott R Sullivan Author") linked in with my experiences in seeing angels and other spiritual encounters. Encouraging words and other goodies on the way.

THE GATE: ETERNITY BECKONS

This book is a fun collection of stories and adventures in God. They speak about how passionate His Love is towards us. Let it bring you joy, hope, and a sense of wonder for all He is. There are also some more difficult stories that will help illuminate how real the spiritual world is, and help build compassion for a lost world.

> *"And it is impossible to please God without faith. Anyone who wants to come to Him must believe that God exists and that he rewards those who sincerely seek Him."* —Hebrews 11:6 NLT

> *"For our present troubles are small and won't last very long. Yet they produce for us a glory that vastly outweighs them and will last forever!"* —2 Corinthians 4:17 NLT

CHAPTER 1

FROM TORMENTED SOUL TO EMPOWERED MAN

"Every good gift and every perfect gift is from above, and comes down from the Father of lights, with whom there is no variation or shadow of turning." — James 1:17 NKJV

I was a normal kid with an "abnormal" gift. I was from a small town—a real small town. The place where I grew up had about 1,000 people in it, with a sleepy blinking yellow light in the middle of main street. It had one grocery store and one school. Entertainment was all about playing outdoors or going to the local pizza restaurant. It was a quiet place, and nowhere special. I loved riding my bike, playing with toys, hanging out with my dog, building forts, and climbing trees. My dog was my best friend and we did everything together. I was a lonely kid and was often picked on and bullied in school. I definitely felt like an outsider and that I really didn't fit anywhere. I never caused trouble in school or life in general, but I was always happy to finish the school day, and come home to my furry friend. Confidence was definitely not a strength of mine and getting bullied daily in school didn't help build it either. Like most kids, I wrestled with self-esteem, and overcoming peer pressure was an uphill climb.

My "gift" was seeing in the spirit and I hated it. It was a constant torment and most days I asked God to take it from me. Most people would not know I ever saw anything. With the "gift," God also gave me a deep strength to walk it out. I think seeing so vividly in the spirit helped me early on to identify that there was True Good and real evil.

Perspective is everything. Have you ever heard a story from two to three different people and they all have a different take on the same facts to the story they heard and/or saw? They may have all had the same experiences, but their unique sets of eyes, ears, and internal filters can shape the way they explain and/or experience that particular situation. Now, no one's experience in that situation is necessarily wrong: it's just different. If we as human beings can have different experiences and perceptions of situations, it is absolutely important that we truly have the One's perspective of every situation in our lives. Our perspectives can be wrong and our own internal filters can be a rudder that turns our life the wrong way.

When we are left to our own devices, we can come up with lots of thoughts, feelings, and imaginations of what the situations in our lives are dictating to us or telling us. This is why seeking Wisdom is everything. If you don't have Wisdom, you will not have the correct perspective or know the right way to turn.

> *"There is a path before each person that seems right, but it ends in death."* —Proverbs 14:12 NLT

Wisdom teaches and shows us the right way to go and the right way to look at situations in our lives, so we hear God's best for us. Seeing in the Unseen World has required great Wisdom on how to walk out the situations. Sometimes the things I have seen are very intense and can be scary. I know for sure that without that Wisdom, I would not be here to write this book.

I clearly remember the first experience I ever had with the Unseen World. I was five years old and just like many five-year-old boys, I was full of adventure, loved roughhousing, playing outside, and riding my bike. I went through most days without a care in the world. One day that suddenly changed when I decided to go up into my attic to find a toy I really wanted. When I opened the door, I had a sense that I shouldn't go there. That sense lingered for a minute, but my desire for the toy and overall curiosity overran it. I walked up the creaky wood steps, sligl ly curved to the right, that led to an all-wood floor and sharp A-frame ceilir I started to look for my toy when suddenly I felt very afraid. Something as in there with me, something very scary. I could not see it, I only felt it: old presence. I remember feeling physically paralyzed, and all I could do s stand and stare straight ahead, as my little knees trembled. Suddenly, a f ire began to take shape. It was a ghoulish figure, small, dark gray, almost t color of ash. It had piercing red eyes, long black fingernails, bony hands, t wings, long tail, and an insidious, terrifying, fanged grin.

I remember standing ther frozen, I couldn't speak, and almost couldn't move. I tried not to look at it ut strangely enough, it had an enticement to it that pulled my eyes towards . The demon spoke to my mind that if I told anybody, it would hurt me an I was very afraid of it hurting me. Suddenly, my legs regained some strengtl nd I ran downstairs and did not tell anybody what happened that day. Tim went on and I was always afraid of that attic, very afraid. The attic door sat st across the hallway from where my bedroom was. I knew I saw something ery evil and very dark. It had all the power and I had none.

A couple years later I was eaded to bed for the night. I shared a room with my little sister and I was (the top bunk. Bunk beds are so fun; I always wanted to be a top bunker. I lc d climbing the ladder each night and sleeping up high. It felt like an advent e. This night was not an adventure I wanted. I was just about asleep, when e door slowly opened. I felt startled, because everyone in the house was asl(and I wasn't sure who would be coming in. My worst fears came to be as t t creature I'd seen in the attic walked into my room. It looked right at me d its face was filled with hate and pride. It knew it had all the power ove ne. I was so afraid I didn't know what to do and I didn't know what to say. was a little boy, so I just hid under the blankets and shook until I fell asl( ). Sadly, that same event would happen frequently throughout my time 1 that house. Each time it would enter my room, terrify me, threaten m(and I would just shake until I feel asleep. I never told anyone, for fear of 1at it would do to me.

THE GATE: ETERNITY BECKONS

A couple of years went by and we moved to a new home. I was ten years old and excited for the new adventure, new room, and new house. It was a nice home with a big yard and, for the first time, I had my own bedroom. It was a downstairs basement bedroom where I could have my own space with no one around, just me and my toys. I loved to set up great adventures with my toy cars, robots, or dinosaurs. I was an introverted kid and very tender-hearted towards others, animals, and even the things I was given. I cared about each toy and I never wanted them to get scratched or broken. That mindset towards people, animals, and even things came to be a very important mindset later on and throughout my life. God really wants us to care about the little things. The little things matter: the little choices of our hearts matter, and the quiet thoughts inside matter because He sees them all.

I got all settled into my new bedroom. It had been a while since I had an experience like I did with the thing in the attic. In fact, I thought with moving away, that creature was no longer going to be around and I didn't have to worry about it anymore. I could not have been more wrong. One night after having a fun-filled day, it was time for bed. I got my jammies on, told my parents goodnight, and off to bed I went. I walked downstairs and into my bedroom, closed the door, turned off the lights, crawled into bed, and closed my eyes to go to sleep.

That night I was not going to get much sleep. I heard a deep breathing in the room; I was suddenly so afraid I felt paralyzed. A set of eyes appeared in my closet, red, just like before. This time though, I saw multiple sets of eyes. Each set of eyes began to show the hideous face it belonged to. Each demon was a different shape and size, but all had the same common thread. All their faces were laced with pride and insidious fanged grins. They knew they had absolute power over me, I couldn't move. I was so afraid and I didn't know what to do. Just like before, I did the only thing I knew to do. I pulled the sheet over my head, balled my knees up to my chest, and shook until I fell asleep.

That night opened a window of time that was very tormenting to my soul. I didn't see the demons every night, but I never knew when I would.

Just like before, they threaten(me with my life if I talked and told anyone. I became so increasingly afra that I would try to sleep with the light on. That didn't work either, and s ne nights, sheets would be pulled off my bed or the light turned off. Othe ights, I would feel breath in my face or hear noises in my room, like scratc g or growling. They were always threatening and I felt that I was their slav and could never escape. It got so bad that I could no longer sleep downst: s and had to sleep on our living-room couch because at night I was just t afraid. My parents didn't understand and thought I was just having nigh ares like many kids do. These were not night- mares of sleep, these were livin ightmares that would torment me any chance they got.

I remember feeling at this ung age that if I talked about what I was ex- periencing, people would thir I was crazy. Maybe they would think some- thing was mentally wrong h me. Or maybe they would think I was emotionally unbalanced or jus ad a big imagination. None of that was true, I was of a sound mind, but I w a tormented soul and very afraid every night that they were coming to get r . It got worse, I started having experiences in the daytime as well. I would lk downstairs to go to my bedroom and feel a hand on my back or breath my neck. Threatening words of death and torment would be whispered i my ears. Sometimes it would be that an over- whelming sense of fear woul grab me so strongly that I had a hard time breathing. I was so sensitive d tender, but somehow, someway, all of this was still not breaking me. I di not know Jesus, but somehow God's strength was there. I would still have f on my bike, running in the park, or playing with my dog. I had normal wing-up activities every day, but I started to feel more and more isolated in de. I knew what I was experiencing was real but I also knew that I didn't k w anyone who would understand it. I knew I needed and wanted help, bu vhere do you look for such a thing as this?

A couple of years went by nd the torment just continued to ratchet up. I would see these beings in full vil, gruesome detail. Each demon's look, def- initely reflected the sin they en yed perpetrating. Some had very thin bodies, with human-like faces, while ers were much more animal in their appear- ance. Some displayed red eye nd some displayed bulged yellow eyes. They all had bat wings, most had tails and long bony fingers with vicious black nails. They all were filled with pride and had those insidious fanged grins. I knew they were not ghosts. In fact, I never questioned if they were ghosts in any way nor do I believe in ghosts at all. They do not exist and are only demons masquerading. Don't play with ghosts or you are welcoming into your life the very things I just described. Think you can play with tarot cards or Ouija boards? I had a relative who thought he could too; he was even given power to levitate tables, by the evil spirits that were invited. A few years later they took his life. Don't play with that stuff at all, ever. Because evil was dabbled with, it opened the door and created a generational curse that fell onto my life. I never touched Ouija boards or tarot cards, but they were enjoyed in my family line and hence came down as a generational curse that I had to overcome.

These spirits were the essence of evil and they only wanted to torment and hurt me. At about 12 years of age I was invited to go to a youth group at a Baptist Church. My friend told me they played a bunch of sports and games there and that it was a ton of fun. I thought, why not give it a try? I went that night and had a really nice time playing basketball and foosball. After the games were over, we were all invited to take a seat and listen to a man give a message. That message changed everything. He spoke about this man named Jesus, and heard about how He died on a cross to save me because I could not save myself. He went on to say that without His sacrifice I was headed to an eternity of torment, but with Him I could know peace and have life everlasting.

Well, that resonated. I certainly knew what torment felt like! I wanted to know more; I needed to know more. I continued to go to that youth group the next couple of years and loved every time I went. It became my weekly escape and the one night of the week I got really excited about. It was interesting that the nights I went to youth group were the same nights that I didn't get any tormenting visitors. I started going more and more. I attended a second night when they opened it up on an additional day in the week. I went to their campouts, game nights, and any event they planned. Every time I went, life and hope got a deeper and deeper grip within me. It came at just the right time, because the 3l nightmares I had in my bedroom had made me feel so trapped, lost, confi ed, broken, and very, very afraid. I was borderline depressed, and I had t ughts of suicide often. I didn't know it then, but I certainly do now, that th uicidal thoughts were just one more way these evil spirits were trying to destr me. The thoughts of suicide always felt like a temptation more than a hop ul escape.

The evil visitors didn't sto coming, but the more I went to youth group and listened to the Word of (d, they didn't come as often. With this new dynamic in my life, balance b an to come into view. Agreement is the gateway to the spiritual world. V o you listen to and what you chose to agree with opens up darkness or lig , evil or goodness, demons or God Almighty over your life.

The more I heard about J us and the truth He spoke, the more I knew He was my way out of this h ible torment I had suffered. I didn't know it at the time, but the Holy Spi was illuminating the path of life to me and guiding me so gently towards

"Your word is a lamp t guide my feet and a light for my path."
—Psalms 119:105 NL

I was 14 now and I went bed one night and it was the worst night of torment I had ever faced. It s ted with a demon grabbing my leg and I felt its cold hand and piercing nail queeze into me. Thoughts of death, gruesome images, and hate coursed thro h my mind. It was as though his very essence was penetrating me. Then m ed sheet was pulled off and I heard growling over top of me. Hot breath wr ped around my neck and I saw demons dancing all around my room. It fe like this was the end, and somehow I knew if they won I would have to liv with these beasts forever. "Something" (the kind Holy Spirit) gave me bol ourage and strength. For the first time, I was able to speak out loud the nan of Jesus and I asked a simple thing: "Jesus, if You are truly real, please save this night. Please save me from the eternity that I'm going to face living h these creatures. I know I've sinned and I know You died on the Cross r me. Please forgive me for my sin. Please come into my life; save me." oom! Just like that, everything changed. I was filled up with a Peace and a Presence like I had never felt before. That same moment the spirits left my room with absolute suddenness. I was free, but I knew there was so, so much more.

I woke up the next morning feeling so alive, so free. Not all of the fear and depression were gone, but something major had changed. For the first time, these creatures were afraid of something. They were pushed around and very, very terrified of Jesus. I didn't know what to do with that, or totally what it all meant. I sure enjoyed having a good night's sleep for the first time in a very long time. The next day, a still, small voice talked to my inner man. He introduced Himself as the Holy Spirit. He spoke quietly to my heart and told me He was going to show me great things: how to know Jesus more, and how to overcome these demons. Every time He spoke to me, it was like a soothing oil on my soul, or that feeling of eating warm bread with lightly melted butter on a cold day. He was so comforting, and not like any voice I had ever heard before. He spoke with a great Authority, but with such incredible levels of tenderness. I knew He was Absolute and I knew obedience to Him would bring life. The change in my life was so sudden and freeing, I chased Jesus with every fiber of my being because I knew He was the Way, the Truth, and the Life, just like He said He was in John 14:6.

The Holy Spirit showed me that the number-one way to know Jesus more was by reading the Bible. With this incredible change in my life, He didn't need to tell me twice. I totally devoured the Word. I read it every day and I wanted to know everything I could. I started in the Book of John because one of my youth leaders advised me that was a good book to start with. All through the Book of John there is story after story of Jesus casting out demons. That was so fascinating to me. Not only was it fascinating because He did it, but now I know that this is normal and He handles these problems on a regular basis. I was powerless my whole life. I was filled with fear, night after night, and in that one moment when Jesus arrived on the scene, demons fled, no questions asked.

I think because of the intensity of my experiences up to this point, the Holy Spirit didn't do anything slow with me. In fact, He drove me deep into the Word quickly to show me hat Authority was all about and how to overcome darkness. It wasn't unt years later that I heard about Paul's teaching referring to the milk of the Wo d and the meat of the Word. The Holy Spirit took me straight to the meat of he Word, and I gladly followed. I knew agreeing with Him was the new ga I wanted open in my life, so all others would close. Within days of accepti Jesus in my heart, the Holy Spirit began to speak to me about the power the blood of Jesus. That was a heavy-hitting conversation and He did not ll punches. He said it's by the blood of Jesus, knowing His Word, and by yo r testimony that true victory will come, over the darkness and demons that ave come to hurt you.

> *"And they have defeated m by the blood of the Lamb and by their testimony. And they di ot love their lives so much that they were afraid to die."* —Revel on 12:11 NLT

When Jesus was on the C ss, He spoke the words, "It is finished." Not only did He make a Way for lvation, but He destroyed all the power of demons and darkness with on swift move. In fact, it says in the Word that He actually openly mocked th rincipalities and darkness while He was hanging on the Cross. They were ver able to have Him turn to selfishness and sin and in His weakest mome He destroyed and took away all their power. He owns the keys to death an ell. No matter what your situation is, or how alone you might feel, there is Savior Who can rescue you from the deepest pit and make you His forever. My pit was dark and deep, but He found me there, just as I was. I didn't cl myself up first; I just called out and He was right there. What are you wa ing for? Let Hope come in now and see the course of your life change.

At this point in my life I d n't have that full understanding of Who Jesus was and what He had truly a omplished on the Cross. I was newly saved teenager. I had a bunch to lea and the most important choice I could make was to be teachable. Now lis n to me here: youth does not qualify you or disqualify you from walking i the power of the Holy Spirit, or to walk with Jesus' Authority, or to chang piritual atmospheres. The only qualifier to those things is one simple wor surrender. The Holy Spirit already knew how little I knew. He only wanted that one thing from me. "Will you surrender to Me? Will you surrender to everything I ask of you? Will you surrender your will, your desires, potentially your life, to find your purpose, your destiny, and why you were created?" Those questions are awesomely soul-shaking. Following Jesus will cost you something— it may cost you everything— but the payout is, and will be well worth the investment. Heaven and Eternity with Him is on the line.

When the Holy Spirit began questioning me, I knew that the course of my life would forever be different. Like I was saying, I was a young man and I didn't know what I was doing. Even though youth group was great, I still had never spoken about what I saw, so I didn't know anybody I could go to and talk to about these things. Yes, I could talk to people about Jesus and the Bible, but I quickly found that not everybody recognizes or even wants to talk about the spiritual realm. I could not understand that on the smallest of levels, considering what I had to live with and walk out. So what do I do now? I'm a new person: I felt peace in my life for the first time, but I wasn't necessarily accepted nor understood anywhere.

After accepting Jesus into my life, I started to see in the spiritual world more than ever before. Before, it was only at night, and evil held all the power. Now I saw demons on people, in stores, on buildings, and flying in the sky. I saw in incredible detail and definition. Having no one to talk to was where the Holy Spirit really set Himself apart as my best Friend, trusted Companion, a Counselor, my Guide, and the One Who would empower me with the courage to overcome these demons and darkness. I was still afraid of confronting those things and I hoped I could find someone I could open up to who would truly understand what I had gone through. My spiritual eyes were awakening more and more, and I could not wait around to find the right person, so I went to the one Friend I always knew told me the truth and helped me.

"I'm going to teach you about Authority," the Holy Spirit said. "You need to understand how Authority works and why you need it in your life," He continued. "You also need to understand that this Authority does not come from you and it is not some t   l that you will use to bring glory to yourself. Authority binds up darkness a   l makes known Jesus' Kingdom and Dominion. So let's start just in your r   om and let's take Authority over these demons that have been tormenting yo   '

"I'm very afraid, though,"   said.

"I know you are, but all y   have to do is speak the words I tell you with Jesus' Name and by His bloo   nd they will obey." He had me stand in the center of my bedroom with my   Bible open and He led me to several Scriptures to speak out against the enem   He showed me immediately that we never war in our own words or our   wn effort. Doing that is senseless because it has no power. The enemy k   ws that and will allow you to move in your own strength, but he won't m   e at all. The enemy will actually gain a deeper grip if you step out in your   n abilities. Ever heard of the seven sons of Sceva? Check out Acts 19:13   -17 and see how well that turned out. Jesus' Name is not something to be   yed with, nor is the spiritual world.

The Holy Spirit showed   that when Jesus was tempted in the wilderness, the Son of God used Sc   ture when warring against Satan. That was very profound to me because J   us, Who created all things spoke the Word to show us how to fight. "Okay,   eak those Scriptures I gave you and command them to go in Jesus' Name,"   e Holy Spirit said. My knees were knocking because I could feel the demo   in my room. I wasn't about to pick a fight with them unless I knew that   ght was going to end in victory for me. The torment that I had gone throu   was real and I was very afraid to take a stand against a foe that had domina   d me my whole life. The Holy Spirit was so gentle, yet strong and firm, t   peak out the Word of God, in Jesus' Name. So that's what I did, and for tl   first time, I experienced victory through His Name. I didn't hide under n   sheets and hope I got through the night. I stood there amazed at my ne   Friend and how He cared so deeply for me. Not only was He there for me   He understood me and wanted me free.

"Look, I have given you   uthority over all the power of the enemy,
and you can walk amo   snakes and scorpions and crush them.
Nothing will injure you.   —Luke 10:19 NLT

"Likewise the Spirit also helps in our weaknesses. For we do not know what we should pray for as we ought, but the Spirit Himself makes intercession for us with groanings which cannot be uttered. Now He who searches the hearts knows what the mind of the Spirit is, because He makes intercession for the saints according to the will of God. And we know that all things work together for good to those who love God, to those who are the called according to His purpose. For whom He foreknew, He also predestined to be conformed to the image of His Son, that He might be the firstborn among many brethren. Moreover whom He predestined, these He also called; whom He called, these He also justified; and whom He justified, these He also glorified. What then shall we say to these things? If God is for us, who can be against us? He who did not spare His own Son, but delivered Him up for us all, how shall He not with Him also freely give us all things? Who shall bring a charge against God's elect? It is God who justifies. Who is he who condemns? It is Christ who died, and furthermore is also risen, Who is even at the right hand of God, Who also makes intercession for us. Who shall separate us from the love of Christ? Shall tribulation, or distress, or persecution, or famine, or nakedness, or peril, or sword? As it is written:

> *'For Your sake we are killed all day long;*
> *We are accounted as sheep for the slaughter.'*

Yet in all these things we are more than conquerors through Him who loved us. For I am persuaded that neither death nor life, nor angels, nor principalities, nor powers, nor things present, nor things to come, nor height, nor depth, nor any other created thing, shall be able to separate us from the love of God which is in Christ Jesus our Lord." —Romans 8:26–39 NKJV

CHAPTER 2

SMALL BEGINNINGS CAN LEAD TO BIG ON-RAMPS

Divorce is a terrible thing ven under the best circumstances. Whether you're part of the splitting cc ple, the children, extended family, or just a friend, everyone gets affected divorce, and rarely in a positive way. In my life I've known many people the various categories listed above who have never recovered from divorce. My parents did get a divorce, and it definitely had a profound effect on the urse of my life and what God was calling me to do. I was 19 at the time an I'd been dating a girl for a couple years and I was really thinking it would l d to marriage. I met her in youth group and even though I was still young narriage was always top of my list of things I desired in my life and that I f called to do. God put it in my heart to work with Him to put an end to th enerational curses of both lines of my family, and dig a generational line of essing with Him. I am not going to get into the details of generational ble ngs vs. generational curses, but both are very powerful and should be unde ood. I would advise studying Deuteronomy. Like I said before, the Holy S rit took me straight to the meat of the Word so true, full freedom could be ved out.

Having unity in family v something I deeply desired. As my family was crumbling around me, I v ited, and I thought I needed, the relationship with my girlfriend to be all th more successful. I was in it to marry her, but her family was moving away d without warning, she suddenly and unexpectedly ended the relationship. My emotions at this time in life were in a really bad place. Family splitting apart, having to move out of the house I grew up in, and now my girlfriend ending the relationship. I felt very unstable and insecure for sure. I had come a long way over the last several years. I was learning more and more about becoming free, all the while seeing in the spirit more and more. I was gaining confidence, but when instability started to take a deeper grip in homelife, insecurity came knocking on my hearts door. Even when our families don't get along or when terrible things are going on in the midst of them, we hope to find some sense of security and belonging. During this time, I didn't feel like I belonged anywhere, not with my family, not with my girlfriend, not at my youth group, and not even in the hometown where I lived. I honestly did not know where my life was headed.

I found myself at the Pittsburgh Airport flying back from the final conversation that ended my relationship with my girlfriend. I had just flown down south to visit her and where her family had moved. I was very sad and I knew that I still was headed back to the volatile situation of my family splitting apart. Depression knocked at the door of my mind and emotions. Temptations came across my will and emotions, to find happiness in all the wrong ways. "Why not pop a pill, take a drink, sleep around?", the dark voices were saying. "Everyone else is doing it, and if God really loved you, He would not have sent this pain." I had seen demons since I was five years old, so I knew these dark voices only wanted my destruction and not my happiness. That being said, temptations are real, and we have to make real choices to turn to God, even if we don't "feel" good inside. Our own unbridled emotions are fertile ground for temptations to grow into sin and destruction.

> "There is a path before each person that seems right, but it ends in death." —Proverbs 14:12 NLT

> "Only simpletons believe everything they're told! The prudent carefully consider their steps. The wise are cautious and avoid danger; fools plunge ahead with reckless confidence." —Proverbs 14:15–16 NLT

I needed hope—real hop... –the kind that fills you and carries you to a new freedom and anchors you... soul. That's exactly what I received, but not in any way I could have ever a... ed for or imagined. No matter what circumstances we find ourselves in, i... ve turn to The Giver of Hope instead of our own devices and even our own... elves, He will always answer.

> "Give all your worries a... l cares to God, for He cares about you."
> —1 Peter 5:7 NLT

> "Now to Him who is a... to do exceedingly abundantly above all that we ask or think, ac... rding to the power that works in us. . ."
> —Ephesians 3:20 NKJ

Before my next flight, I w... ked into the food court and ordered a simple lunch. I sat down at a long ca... teria table and started to bow my head to give God thanks for the food. As... vas beginning to pray, I saw a man out of my peripheral vision, sitting a cou... le seats away from me. He had slicked-back hair, a black leather jacket, an... a goatee. He was kind of a big, strong, biker-looking dude. I noticed his ja... et especially because I like leather jackets and motorcycles. I bowed my hea... to give thanks, and right when I picked my head up, this stranger in black... ooked over at me and said, "You know, God is going to give you a family s... meday, just like you have been asking Him." It totally stunned me, and I loo... d down trying to gather myself both mentally and emotionally. My head wa... pinning. How could this guy know anything like that? Who was he? I cou... see that he was standing up and walking towards the trash can carrying h... tray. I wanted to say something to him, even a thank you, or maybe ask a... estion. But as I turned my head to speak to him, this physical man vanishe... in front of my eyes! I looked around at everyone else in the food court to s... if anyone was reacting. No one was the least disturbed or even noticed he... d disappeared. I was both astonished and in shock. In that moment the H... y Spirit's still, small voice spoke to my heart: "That was an angel and your... e will never be the same. The most unstoppable force in life is surrender... aith, and obedience. If you do those things, then the Kingdom will come... on you, move around you and through you."

THE GATE: ETERNITY BECKONS

I sat there staring down at my pizza for who knows how long, trying to gather my thoughts at how this angel, came, spoke to me, then disappeared. Who am I to experience something so amazing? The crackling speaker went off over my head, announcing my flight was boarding. I heard my flight number, but the rest sounded like an adult from a Charlie Brown cartoon. I grabbed my bag and with a full heart and forward eyes, wondering what was coming next. A new semester was on the horizon and with that, some of my biggest adventures would begin.

I don't know about you, but school never excited me. I was an okay student and I could have been very good, but I am a visual learner. Probably why God gave me the gift of being a seer. Books and lectures bore me and I wanted something more. After seeing in the spirit for so many years now, everything else felt boring and I struggled with things keeping my attention. It was especially hard when the unseen world peeled open before me and I found myself praying more and more for my life to make sense. What do I do with what I see? What is the purpose?

I had just finished the first two years of community college and I was about to transfer to a university at the time of my Pittsburgh airport experience. I knew this should be a big decision in my life, but for some reason I didn't feel it was as important as knowing what to do with the "disappearing airport man." I had everything set up in my life. All my credits transferred to the local university, if I kept my grades up. I already had a job offer in my field of study. I felt peace about going to school, but something wasn't quite right. I felt peace, but not purpose. I did the only thing I was ever good at, I dropped to my knees and surrendered. You see, the Pittsburgh airport experience was not just seeing an angel; the Holy Spirit was calling me to something bigger and deeper. I just did not know what. As I surrendered school and life direction, His real Peace entered my soul. I knew I was pleasing Him and His answer floored me. Instead of going to the school that I had everything set up with, He spoke quietly to me to do quite the opposite: He asked me to go to the school my now-ex-girlfriend was attending. Not only was nothing set up for that, it was multiple states away, and did I mention my ex-girlfriend went there? "God, people are going to think I am nuts! This is not a financially sound decision. ... o one will understand this." I could go on, but needless to say, I had a boo ... full of excuses for why this was way too much to ask of me. God is always k ... d, but He is God, and His Ways are not our ways. He sees things we do n ... . He knows things we do not, He knows how things will end and where He ... ants our life to go; we do not. Going to His deep place always costs, but t ... t's where Eternity takes shape and destiny is revealed.

After much wrestling and ... onsternation, in my spirit I knew this was of Him, even if my mind and e ... otions were a wreck. So, I obeyed, truly left everything, went to an uncon ... ortable place and chased His presence before me. This was not a mission t ... reconcile with my girlfriend. The Lord had made it clear that was not His ... ill. This was a different mission, that I would understand only after I leaped ... This huge step of faith was linked to the "dis-appearing-man event" in a wa ... I did not understand, but distinctly knew in my spirit. I won't bore you w ... n the events of the first few months, but let's just say I was meeting great p ... ople, enjoying my time, and still very broken over all that had gone on in n ... life. I did not feel strong inside, but I knew I had obeyed Him, that was t ... number-one thing I wanted in my life.

I met a nice girl, and we b ... t a great friendship over several months. One day, I took her on a walk (on \ ... entine's Day) and asked if we could date. She was all in. Whew! Our relati ... ship was great! Tons of fun, but no pressure. This was leading somewhere ... eat, I knew, but I kept that close to the vest. After dating for awhile, I aske ... God for confirmation in both of our hearts if marriage was what He desired ... Once again, He answered me in a way I could not have asked or imagined.

The night was cool, and t ... sky was illuminated by a big beautiful moon. We had a pretty creek that ran ... hrough some wooded area on the back of the campus. It was a great night f ... a walk and that is exactly what my now-girl-friend and I were doing. We v ... re just talking about life and having our usual fun time. Then I saw somethi ... g. Something not nice, and very dark. Before me appeared three sets of holl ... r blue eyes. They looked like animal eyes and felt very dangerous. Their he ... ls were moving and sizing us up. I saw their jaws, filled with sharp, piercing teeth with blood dripping; pure evil was their intent. I looked to the right, and I saw dozens of similar eyes, all holding the same wicked, hate-filled gaze. Before I could say anything, my girlfriend spoke, "Do you see those eyes?"

"Yes, I do." I said. "What kind of animals do you think they are?" she asked. I knew God was protecting her mind in that moment. I simply asked her if I could pray. She agreed, and I prayed, faith-filled, no fear, that God would protect us and keep us safe. He did, and we exited the woods the opposite way of those beasts. On our way out, the Holy Spirit quickened my heart to know they were spirits of murder.

Seeing these demons was intense for sure, but God gave me His incredible grace to walk out of the woods and keep my wits about me. Yes, they were scary, but I was not that little boy anymore, and I knew the power of Jesus in me. What I was really scared of was the coming conversation with a girl I truly loved. We exited the wooded path and were back on campus. This was a major make-or-break moment for our relationship. I knew I had to tell her what they really were and what their intent was. It could have scared her deeply, and she could have run away. Not much had changed from those youth-group days, as far as not really talking about what I see. I would mention things to people here and there to test the water. It was hard to find welcoming water. I saw things and knew things that others did not. I learned to hold it tight to the vest and rely on the Holy Spirit to tell me what to say, to whom, and when. This conversation I was about to have was going to be different. For the first time, I had to tell the whole story and risk losing the relationship with a woman I truly loved. It was a big risk, but if this was leading to marriage, then my wife-to-be, whoever she was, had to know what God had saved me from, and what He was calling me to. The Cross comes with cost and we have to be willing to pay it. God is not cruel, but He is a jealous God and wants to be our first love. I spotted a bench under a bright streetlight, and thought that would be a good place to have this conversation. My heart was beating hard; I sat next to her and began to gently share the full detail of what I saw. She cried deeply and said nothing, her head hung low.

I walked her back to her dorm I went to mine, not sure where to go next or if we would continue to walk together.

A Fu -Circle Friend

A few years had passed si e that day in the airport. I was now married to that wonderful woman wh n I talked to on that bench in college. She was the perfect fit for me. Go had spoken to her heart and explained to her the calling He had for me and at what I experienced was more real than the natural world around us. We vere the best of friends. God had heard my heart's cry and blessed me!

My childhood dog had p sed away by this time. Of course I was very sad, but God had blessed me th a lifelong best friend and life was great. I loved animals so much and I w ited my new wife to experience the friendship I had growing up. She agreed, nd wanted to get a couple of cats and see how it went. Of course, it took no ime for her to fall in love and enjoy how fun animals can be.

We were just getting star d, newly married, and having so much fun. We both worked, and each Fri y night we always went out on a date. Some- times we went to the mall, sa a movie, grabbed some dinner—just normal date stuff. This particular Fri y night was like any other as we left to go on our date. What appeared as a t ally normal night, suddenly shifted to another life-changing event. We went o a movie at our favorite $1.50 cheap movie theater. We watched a fun fl k and when it ended, we proceeded towards the exit. We noticed no work around and saw another movie was just get- ting started. We both looked each other and thought, what harm can come from sneaking into another m vie that we didn't pay for? Remember how I mentioned earlier that God ca s about the little things? Little choices matter to Him because it shows whe our character is and if He can trust us with more. We looked twice, then uickly darted in. We lasted 10 minutes: the movie was awful and evil. D ons speak through movies and television all the time. It's an easy way to en the door to their activity in our lives. We knew we had sinned and that we had displeased God. We quickly asked for His forgiveness and vowed never to steal again.

Coming back from our date, we headed into our apartment to close out the day. We did all our normal stuff of getting pajamas on, brushing our teeth, fluffing our pillows, and climbing into bed. As my wife and I lay there in bed, chatting about the night, a dark presence entered the room. I could see the demon in full color. He had three other spirits with him, menacing with a sense of stubbornness. He knew he had a right to be there and was not planning on leaving. I knew he had come because we opened that door by exposing ourselves to that evil movie. My heart broke. I did not want to fail that way or ever give an opportunity to those things again. I tried to cast it out, but it wasn't working. Instead, the Holy Spirit spoke to me and said: "Your choice opened this door. Be repentant and worship, then it will be closed." We asked God for forgiveness again with true contriteness. I asked my wife to begin to worship and sing. It didn't leave right away, but the more we worshiped, the more the atmosphere changed. Suddenly the Holy Spirit's presence became very thick in the room. I saw a golden light pour into our place and wash the demons right out. I knew I was seeing the Holy Spirit. His golden light invaded our bedroom and I could feel Him all around. My body began to shake and my eyes began to see a vision from Heaven. I could see through the roof of our apartment complex and I saw angels everywhere, blowing trumpets. It seemed there were a couple hundred angels. There was a great swirling of incredible blue light in the sky as I heard resounding vocal worship in the air.

One of the angels descended into our apartment and introduced himself as Jonathan. He gave his Heavenly name first, but it's a language that cannot be pronounced by a human tongue. He wasn't overly big, maybe 5 9 tall, blue eyes, sandy-brown hair, sword in a sheath hanging from a golden belt around his waist. He wore a tunic and golden sandals on his feet. His eyes and face were filled with kindness, and in that moment he reminded me of my experience in the Pittsburgh Airport.

He told me, "I was the man in the black leather jacket."

What? You don't look any ıing like him, I thought. I didn't dare ask this out loud of course, because aı ngel was standing in my bedroom talking to me! Haha!

He spoke to me that I hac ıeen set aside and called of the Lord. He said the Lord placed a birthmark oı he back of my head that means blessed, righteous, called. It blew me away Who was I? From a no-place town, never accomplished anything big in n life, poor most of my life, but God looks on the inside.

"You are called, you have destiny, and a great purpose! Don't compare yourself to others, seek Him o know all of who you were made to be," Jonathan said.

I looked back up through ıy apartment ceiling and saw all those angels continuing to worship. I saw c uds rolling in, and a figure sitting on a Throne appeared within the clouds. l ı head raced with questions, but as the Holy Spirit fell more and more in (r bedroom, I fell into a deep sleep. When I awoke the next morning, my :ar loving wife, filled with faith, came to me and said, "That was incredibl Do you know you shook for over two hours and the Holy Spirit spoke thrc gh you to me and prophesied about our life?" Joyful bounciness was a norma ıtate of being for my wife, but this was on another level, especially pre-cofl . As I gathered my thoughts and drank my coffee, we discussed the whole ıight and how much our lives would never be the same.

> "The thief comes only to ıal and kill and destroy. I came that they may have Life and have abundantly." —John 10:10 ESV

> "To You, O Lord, I lift ı my soul. O my God, I trust in You; Let me not be ashamed; Let ıt my enemies triumph over me. Indeed, let no one who waits on u be ashamed; Let those be ashamed who deal treacherously with t cause. Show me Your ways, O Lord; Teach me Your paths. ı ıd me in Your truth and teach me, For You are the God of my ı lvation; On You I wait all the day. Remember, O Lord, Your ı ıder mercies and Your loving kindnesses,

For they are from of old. Do not remember the sins of my youth, nor my transgressions; according to Your mercy remember me, for Your goodness' sake, O Lord. Good and upright is the Lord; therefore He teaches sinners in the way. The humble he guides in justice, And the humble He teaches his way. All the paths of the Lord are mercy and truth, to such as keep his covenant and His testimony. For Your name's sake, O Lord, pardon my iniquity, for it is great. Who is the man that fears the Lord? Him shall he teach in the way he chooses. He himself shall dwell in prosperity, his descendants shall inherit the earth." —Psalm 25:1–14 NKJV

CHAPTER 3

CAN'T DANCE; SURE CAN FLY

Several years later during summertime, my wife and I were living in Western New York state. Our marriage continued to grow and we often experienced the supernatural. Sometimes I would see a demon on someone in a store, or an angel ministering to a young child. Seeing in the spirit was a daily occurrence for me and my wife and I always sought the Lord for wisdom on how to walk out each situation. He worked within us a deep sensitivity in the spirit and love toward others, so we could partner with Him in all He wanted to accomplish. We are His hands and feet, and He deeply wants to move through us to bring His Kingdom into this fallen world.

I woke up one morning, got a cup of coffee and headed off to work. As I continued on my drive, I felt a nagging impression inside that God wanted to talk to me about something. I knew we weren't settled where we lived, and I knew He had something more for our lives. Humanly, we can imagine a lot, dream a lot, and have many thoughts as to where our life is headed and what our best scenario might be. I had no idea what He wanted to talk about, but I knew I must quiet myself and begin to listen. I've discovered, throughout my life, that our thoughts are so much smaller than His thoughts and our plans so much smaller than His plans.

Then He dropped it: "I want to move you to Florida. I have something for you to accomplish there and do for Me."

The Gate: Eternity Beckons

What? Florida? Why would I want to go to Florida? Well, I do live in gray overcast skies, in winter eight months out of the year, so sunshine year around and palm trees doesn't sound too painful.

"The price will be high and I need you to go right away."

I still get the palm trees, right?

It is so true that when God asks us to do something, there's always a cost, there's always faith, and we always have a choice. He doesn't always ask us to do things that work around our sense of convenience. He doesn't ask us to obey when the time is just right for us. He wants our hearts surrendered and our will reaching for Him. So I'm just like you, at a crossroads of obedience, surrender, choice, and my personal convenience and desire for control. Am I willing to lay it all down? I would love to tell you after previous angelic encounters and shakings from the Holy Spirit, that obedience is automatic. It never is, it never will be, and we have to lay our desires down for His best.

More often than not, God has asked me to jump into the dark with little to no instructions, as He lays out His perfect plan. Do you know He moves this way purposely? It forces us to trust in His Goodness over our emotions. I have not mastered this, but my goal is that my speed in obedience increases more and more as His call continues for more. The Holy Spirit is always on the move and we have to learn to move with Him and not depend on our own wisdom. Our wisdom will cause us to look with our earthly eyes and it will fail us every time. His wisdom gives us a glimpse into how Heaven works and it will never fail.

> *"The Message that points to Christ on the Cross seems like sheer silliness to those hellbent on destruction, but for those on the way of salvation it makes perfect sense. This is the way God works, and most powerfully as it turns out. It's written, I'll turn conventional wisdom on its head, I'll expose so-called experts as foolish. So where can you find someone truly wise, truly educated, truly intelligent in this day and age? Hasn't God exposed it all as pretentious nonsense? Since the world in all its fancy wisdom never had a clue*

when it came to knowin___ God, God in his wisdom took delight in
using what the worl___ considered dumb—preaching, of all
things!—to bring those ___ ___o trust Him into the way of salvation."
—1 Corinthians 1:18–___ ___ MSG

I could go into all the di___ ___og my wife and I had about this upcoming move, but let's just say we we___ back and forth on all the pros and cons and all the reasons we should go a___ ___ all the reasons we should stay. If you're any-thing like me, I'm sure you al___ ___ady know what those conversations are like. And honestly, it's not about the___ ___onversations; it's about the choice that follows those conversations.

So here we were, not sitt___ ___ on a big bank account, driving to Florida, and to a particular town in Fl___ ___ida I did not know anything about. He said go, and we want to live surrenc___ ___ed lives, so we did. There was no great parade waiting for us, no applause, ___ ___ celebration, no chanting our names saying, "You are people of great faith! ___ ___n fact, no one had a clue about that conver-sation we had with the Holy ___ ___irit. Even when we arrived in Florida, there was no clear roadmap of what ___ ___e were to do. We waited on God and he di-rected our steps to a church t___ ___t honored Him, and that's where a true ad-venture began.

A few months went by, we ___ ___oth were working, and had found a nice place to live. We were serving at the ___ ___urch, and we were still waiting to know what the real reason was that we we___ ___ here. There was fruit in our lives, we felt we were making an impact at the ___ ___urch and at our jobs, but something greater was tugging at my heart.

My wife has an incredible ___ ___ift of faith. By the way, that is extremely im-portant to find in a spouse. I___ ___d someone who loves Jesus more than he or she loves you, then you will b___ ___loved from the right place. My wife is like a stork, so no matter how high ___ ___he flood water gets, her legs are always long enough to stand above it. Iron___ ___ally, my wife is very short, but her faith stands taller than any of the trees aro___ ___nd her. She is also like a duck; though she is in the water, she floats on to___ ___nd the water rolls off her back. Not much ever gets to her.

I'm entirely different. My emotions fluctuate up and down, I want to know the answer and find out the why, so God typically answers me in a unique and different ways to keep me guessing. We have different gifts, and hence we function in our walk with God very differently. We prayed early on that the Holy Spirit would help us identify our personalities, gifts, and talents. We asked Him that as He reveals those gifts, He would show us how to reflect Him through the gifts and bring oneness to our marriage. That's another topic for another day, so back to our story.

Our church decided to have a four-day conference and invited a guest speaker. At this point in our Florida adventure, I was not feeling so adventurous. I was feeling more worried about all our life circumstances. Did I really hear from You correctly? Maybe I missed something; maybe I got it wrong. Yes, our life was better, we were happier, but that wasn't the reason we were asked to come here. We were sent for a purpose.

I was beginning to be excited about this four-day conference. I had not heard of the guest speaker before, but he was coming to share on how to hear God deeper. Well, I need two scoops of that! Do you love ice cream? Boy, I sure do, with a little whipped cream and sprinkles. Yummy! Sorry, dessert distracts. Back to our story.

The first day of the conference had arrived and the house was packed. There was an electricity in the air and I felt the excitement. God was going to show up. The speaker's name was Elias, and he began to share words of knowledge, wisdom, prophetic words, and several people were healed. It was amazing! If you have never been around those things, please do! It's so important to experience God in His fullness. My heart raced, and I asked God in desperation to please give me a word, anything so that I would know I made the right choice coming here. I wanted Him to confirm that He has a real plan for us. I was always willing to take risks, but for some reason it got harder after we were married. Probably because I knew there was more on the line. God, knowing all of that, made me take more risks; I guess He thought I needed the practice. Haha!

The first night of the con ence passed with nothing specific happening for me, then the second day thing, and the third day nothing. Each day was incredibly impactful an people's lives were absolutely, powerfully changed. I had never been aro id anything like it before and I was astounded to see the gifts of the Holy Sp t at work. Total peace, total love, for all who received. I continued to ask (d to speak, but I didn't hear from Him in my spirit. God had also shut my res off to seeing in the spirit during the conference. The sneaky Holy Sp t, was up to something. . . well. . . sneaky. We were at the fourth day of tl conference and there was going to be a morning- and an evening session. I as at the morning session and again God was moving powerfully. People's li s were continuing to be changed. I didn't get a word, and now a bit of disa ointment and discouragement was crowding in around my soul.

After the morning session, veral of us went out to lunch. As I was sitting there eating lunch with my fi nds, I looked over and I saw all the pastoral staff sitting together with the uest speaker, Elias. People at my table were still eating as the pastoral staff the other table finished and started to leave. The restaurant was very long id as the last of the pastoral staff exited the building, Elias was following hind. He stopped at the front doors, turned around, looked me straight in e eyes and started walking towards me. I was so nervous! You can't be looki at me, right? Oh, he sure was and he walked right up to me.

"Young man, what is you ame?"

I almost forgot my own ime. "Um, Scott Sullivan," I said, as sweat beaded up on my head. With kind and direct gaze, he nodded his head and walked away and out of the res urant. "God, what do I do with that?" I knew it was Him and that the Holy pirit had spoken to Elias, but I didn't understand the results. I felt peace a l a bounce in my step, but once again I found myself waiting for an answer.

The evening session came id the church was the most packed it had ever been. Almost standing room nly. I was excited to be there and I figured I would probably get some type f word given to me but definitely on the sidebar after the service was over. That was totally fine with me and that was totally my hope. The service started, and like every other time, Elias started the service with prophetic words, words of wisdom, words of knowledge, and healings were coming forth throughout the room. It was an amazing experience! And then, just like every other session. it came to a conclusion and now it was time for him to share a message. Every other session we would have this ministry time first and then he would speak a great message. He stepped back and began to get himself ready to deliver the message. Then he stopped and said this "The Holy Spirit is telling me to do something. I am not exactly sure what's going to happen, but we're going to roll with this and see how He moves."

"Well, this should be interesting," I thought.

After three sessions of awesomeness, what new thing would happen? "Is there a young man by the name of Scott Sullivan here?," Elias said. I panicked. I am not an attention seeker and this was not what I was looking for haha! He was looking back and forth from the stage, so I slowly raised my hand, almost hoping he wouldn't see it. "Great. Stand up, come down front and please stand against the far wall in the sanctuary. Now I'm going to stand on the other far wall of the sanctuary and we are going to do exactly what the Holy Spirit has spoken to my heart to do," Elias said. My legs were like jelly, and my heart was beating so fast, yet there was the Holy Spirit's incredible peace.

"This is what we are going to do," Elias said. "The Holy Spirit wants us to walk towards each other and before we meet, the Holy Spirit is going to meet you." He motioned me to walk, and as I started to walk across the front of the sanctuary towards Elias, my legs got so heavy and I felt like I was walking through molasses. Heat came all over my body, and my strength was totally leaving me. The Holy Spirit started to fall more and more on me and I could barely stand. When I got within about five feet of Elias, I was unable to move anymore. I could not take another step. Elias spoke, "The Holy Spirit wants you to know that He will always meet you before the theologies of man."

Now to you that might sound like a strange message to receive, but to me it meant everything in the world. When I first came to know Jesus and accepted Him in my heart, I asked Him to always protect me so that I would never be deceived in the last days. I never shared that with anyone besides my wife, so this was a deeply, deeply personal message. The word penetrated deep into my soul and tears streamed down my face. The weight of His presence was getting incredibly heavy. I began to sway back and forth and I was unable to stop myself as I fell head first towards the carpet. The crowd gasped, but somehow, I was told later, tucked and rolled at the last second. No worries, it didn't hurt. I didn't even feel it. Haha!

As soon as my body struck the floor, my spirit man jumped out of my body. Yes, you read that right and please don't close the book! I had zero experience with this leading up to this event. I had not read about it, I had not heard a teaching about it, but I was out of my body and staring back at my physical body shaking violently on the floor. I can't dance, but my shaking body sure seemed to have a rhythm. I looked into the crowd, but nobody was looking at me. They were looking at my body on the ground. I was filled with a joy that permeated my soul.

I began to worship and then suddenly an angel was standing right next to me. It was Jonathan, whom I had met earlier in my life. With such kindness all over his face he said, 'It's time to go." Just like that, he grabbed my arm and we floated out of church right into the sky. I looked down and saw all the houses, cars, and the church, but I kept going up. Higher and higher we went, until cities were seen like little lights. Suddenly we floated high enough that I could see the shape of the earth. It was a beautiful round marble. Jonathan squeezed my arm a little tighter and we shot off with blinding speed! Stars were whipping past my head and they were just blurs of light. Just as fast as we traveled, we suddenly stopped! Before me I saw a single Gate, curved at the top and fashioned completely out of pearl. To the right stretched a band of clouds and to the left just the same, as far as my eyes could see. The Gate had pearl bars going down the middle and you could see through it. It was spectacular-looking, and light it was piercing through the bars. I knew there was freedom, love, and a huge world beyond that Gate. What struck me the most was that there was a single Gate, no other way to get in and I was instantly reminded of John 14:6: "I Am the Way, I Am the Truth, I Am a Life and no one comes to the Father but through Me."

> *"So Jesus spoke again, I assure you that I am the Gate of the sheep. All who came before me were thieves and outlaws, but the sheep didn't listen to them. I am the Gate. Whoever enters through me will be saved. They will come in and go out and find pasture."*
> —John 10:7–9 GNT

> *"Enter by the narrow gate. For the gate is wide and the way is easy that leads to destruction, and those who enter by it are many. For the gate is narrow and the way is hard that leads to life, and those who find it are few."* —Matthew 7:13–14 ESV

CHAPTER 4

COME AGAIN, WHO'S TALKING?

So here I was standing at the Pearly Gate ready to walk into Heaven. As the Gate opened, Jonathan guided me in. I didn't know what to expect. As we walked in I was awash with the purest of Light. Peace and contentment enveloped me with an embrace of a summer's breeze. Color was reflecting, refracting, and moving all around. Tints, shades, and pure dynamics of the colors were so far beyond anything that Earth could muster. Just by them alone, I knew I was in a place that was so far beyond my mind's ability to comprehend. There were lots of clouds and I knew that the expanse I was standing in was immeasurable. Boundless Eternity was before me. I saw so many flowers of different shapes and sizes. As I looked at them they all looked at me. Yes, you heard that right; they looked at me. If I took a step to the right or left or went straight, they all turned to watch.

Off in the vast distance I saw a light so brilliant I would fail with words to describe it, but here's my best attempt. I saw no form, just a mass of light and I cannot tell you how far away it was, but I knew it was a great, great, great, great distance from where I was. Have you seen pictures from the Hubble Telescope? If you have ever seen a picture from the Hubble telescope of a galaxy and you look at the galaxy's center there are so many stars you cannot see form. That's what the light was like but a trillion times more intense, truly a trillion. I asked Jonathan what it was that I was seeing, and he looked at me and said, "It is the Throne. It where I AM sits."

"The Lord has made the heavens His throne; from there He rules over everything." —Psalms 103:19 NLT

"But the Lord is in his holy Temple; the Lord still rules from heaven. He watches everyone closely, examining every person on earth." ⊦—Psalms 11:4 NLT

I was lost in amazement and wonder as I gazed off, but my eyes turned more towards what was approaching me. I saw a figure coming my way. No, not a figure, but three figures—three very short figures. Like I said before, I had no expectations because I have never been to Heaven before. Furthermore, it's Heaven! How would I know what to expect? Haha! If you would have asked before this trip who I thought I would meet when I went to Heaven, oh, I would probably mention some great Bible character. That was not God's plan for this day.

The figures appeared out of the mist and they were three animals, one dog and two cats, and I knew them all because they used to be mine. The first one I met was my dog Missy, who was my best friend growing up. She was my furry friend who walked with me through all those terrible tormenting nights. She looked at me with kindness in her eyes, and said "I was so glad to be assigned to you, and I was so glad to help you and be your companion." Move your hand, grab your chin, and slowly press up. Yes, animals talk and live in Heaven. I can hear your squeals, all you animal lovers out there. Quick, put the book down, do a happy dance, and make sure you don't bite your tongue when correcting jaw-drop.

Next to approach me was Reeses, one of my cats I picked out with my wife when we were newly married, and she said, "I was so glad to be your friend. I enjoyed supporting you and loving you when you needed it."

Last to approach was Necco, my other cat. She is so sweet, but not so bright. Necco walked right up to me, love in her eyes, and smiled. She turned and said nothing. "Yeah," I thought, "That fits. Ha! Ha!"

God is such a tender loving God; He is all-powerful, but He certainly cares about the little details and all the little things He has made.

"What is the price of two sparrows—one copper coin? But not a single sparrow can fall to the ground without your Father knowing it." —Matthew 10:29 NLT

"And the very hairs on your head are all numbered. So don't be afraid; you are more valuable to God than a whole flock of sparrows." —Luke 12:7 NLT

"For the life of every living thing is in His hand, and the breath of every human being." — Job 12:10 NLT

I stood there trying to process what just happened, and then my eye caught Jonathan motioning me over to a horse with a chariot. It was a beautiful white stallion, with gold [...]tes all over it. The chariot was crafted out of pearl with gold trim around the wheels and in the finest of details. This was the most incredible craftsman ship I had ever laid my eyes on. As I walked towards the horse and chariot, Jonathan said, "It's time for you to see something that is very important."

Jonathan motioned to step into the chariot. I and all my animals stepped in and off we went with an *explosion* of power and light, straight into the sky. Heaven was beautiful—so, so beautiful! The trials we endure cannot match the glory we will see, experience, and walk in.

"Jonathan, we are sure flying fast!"

"I could ask Bill to slow down," he replied.

"I didn't say I wasn't enjoying it. Wait, Bill?"

"That's me. You don't like my flying?" the beautiful white stallion said.

"Oh no, it's great; I just. . . am I talking to a horse?"

"You talked to me," Missy my childhood dog, said.

Danger! Danger! Overload detected in man's small pea brain. Push eject button before meltdown sequence is initiated. Warning! Warning!

Jonathan, with love-filled eyes and an understanding expression, placed his hand on my shoulder. "Shhhh. Just look."

"So then, my beloved brethren, let every man be swift to hear, slow to speak. . ." —James 1:19

The Word still applies in Heaven.

As I gazed out across Heaven, my eyes took in mountains, bodies of water, rivers, valleys, flowers, bridges, walkways, and many, many more sights. Colors were truly out of this world in their brilliance. Textures so rich it makes top-of-the-line HDTVs laughable. A brilliant Light cascaded and washed over everything, Golden and Pure.

As the chariot descended, a breathtaking valley came into full view. It was larger and more magnificent than anything Earth could muster. The valley was so grand in scale one entire side of the valley swept up like a gargantuan ocean wave, but all rock. As we flew past this "rock ocean wave", we started to descend and it became clear we were landing at what appeared to be a construction site. The rocks themselves pulsated with the very essence of Life itself. Just flying by them I could feel His Life Force pump through me. I began to think how wonderful this location of Heaven was, sitting up on a mountain, overlooking an enormous valley with a gargantuan panorama all around. The whole scene felt familiar, but still completely foreign. I would have loved to stay there, just getting lost in the beauty. It felt like a place I could sit for a thousand years with never saying a word. The Peace of that place was the very air that you breathe.

The chariot came to a soft landing. Jonathan and I stepped out and walked over to the construction site. Stone slabs for walls, various log beams for support, a true log-cabin or lodge feel. Angels were wearing construction hats and were busy putting the building together. It was being partially built into the mountain.

"What do you think?" Jonathan asked.

I cried, "It so amazing. It such an incredible-looking place!"

There were words written each rock and carvings in the logs, but I did not recognize the language. construction was somewhat recognizable, yet totally not of the Earth.

"Why is this being built? asked.

"It's being built for you." Jonathan replied. "This is for the work you have done on Earth for His k gdom." I cried. It was so humbling. "Did He not say that He is going prepare a place for you?" All that heartache, the hurt, was so worth pushin through in faith and obedience.

"Wow, wow, wow!! Who n I to receive such goodness?" I said.

Jonathan replied, "You are His son, truly a son. You have been grafted in and abide in the Vine."

No matter who you are o vhere you are, or what circumstances you are facing, the Heavenly Father i calling out to you. He wants you, He loves you, He wants to prepare a pla for you, and have you with Him for all Eternity. You are so loved. You ar not alone, you are seen, by the Greatest set of Eyes that could possibly look you.

We walked over to the sid of the house and I saw a pile of various materials, neatly stacked, but defin ly not being used in the construction. Some were iron and some copper, al many things I did not recognize because they were not of the Earth.

"What are the materials f ?" I asked.

"Oh, those are possibly yo rs. It all depends on the choices you make on Earth in faith and obedience. hey are the choices you have not yet had the opportunity to make. Get rea because you will have decisions to make and they will propel you deeper wi Him. They are not all easy, but they are Eternally worth it. Come, come, eed to show you more. Those gold plates on Bill are not just for decoration

"Let not your heart be troubled; you believe in God, believe also in Me. In My Father's house are many mansions; if it were not so, I would have told you. I go to prepare a place for you. And if I go and prepare a place for you, I will come again and receive you to Myself; that where I am, there you may be also. And where I go you know, and the way you know." —John 14:1–4 ESV

"For ever since the world was created, people have seen the earth and sky. Through everything God made, they can clearly see His invisible qualities—His eternal power and divine nature. So they have no excuse for not knowing God." —Romans 1:20 NLT

"I pray that out of his glorious riches He may strengthen you with power through His Spirit in your inner being, so that Christ may dwell in your hearts through faith. And I pray that you, being rooted and established in love, may have power, together with all the Lord's holy people, to grasp how wide and long and high and deep is the love of Christ, and to know this love that surpasses knowledge—that you may be filled to the measure of all the fullness of God. Now to Him who is able to do immeasurably more than all we ask or imagine, according to His power that is at work within us." —Ephesians 3:16–20 NKJV

CHAPTER 5

I AM

As Jonathan walked me b   k towards Bill, the horse (I am sure he has a much greater name than that, l   t my pea brain was told what it could handle), I found myself a bit stunned   all I was seeing. I marveled at how my life and choices could have such a   impact on what happened in Heaven. I had always seen Heaven as a place   would go after I died, arrive there, and then assimilate into its surrounding   I never really thought about how I was in- fluencing activities and outco   es in this Eternal place. This was vibrating through my spirit as I was ab   rbing the revelation that He already laid the foundation, and paid the price   Now I needed to decide how much I want to believe it all, and run with Hi   . I felt the weight of this new deeply-rooted Eternal perspective. I knew l   vould never look at life the same way again. This was already changing me   d opening my eyes to the truth—that we are just passing through this life a   l that we are ambassadors for His Kingdom.

> *"For we [believers will b   alled to account and] must all appear be-*
> *fore the judgment seat oj   hrist, so that each one may be repaid for*
> *what has been done in t.   body, whether good or bad [that is, each*
> *will be held responsible f   his actions, purposes, goals, motives—the*
> *use or misuse of his time   pportunities and abilities]." "So we are*
> *ambassadors for Christ,   s though God were making His appeal*
> *through us; we [as Chris   representatives] plead with you on behalf*
> *of Christ to be reconciled   God." —2 Corinthians 5:10, 20 AMP*

It was so powerful to see those unused construction materials and realize all the little choices matter. God cares about our character and about how we live. If you really love someone, you do the things that honor that person. Salvation is available by the finished work of the Cross alone. There is no other way, and no amount of good works that can get you into Heaven without giving your life to Christ.

Once we give our lives to Him and accept His salvation, then we need to be living for Him and not of this world. We live, act, talk, and walk differently, because Jesus clearly stated He was not of this world, nor should we be. We have an Eternal call and destiny to be fashioned. Our actions affect our rewards. I don't know about you, but I like presents!

As I began to walk towards Bill, the plates of gold that were on him really caught my attention. They were perfectly crafted to fit his head and shoulders and they shone and glimmered in the Golden Light that permeated the entire atmosphere. The plates were inlaid with precious stones, particularly around his head and down his muzzle. As I moved my hand across the gold, it felt like smooth glass, so pure, so perfectly formed. Then I started to see what Jonathan wanted me to see—names. He wanted me to focus particularly on the muzzle. Written on the crest of Bill's head was "Karla," my wife's name, then several names I did not recognize. I inherently knew they were names, but I could not read the language.

They were written below hers, going down his forehead in a very orderly fashion. Each name had a specific gem embedded next to it.

"Jonathan, who are they?"

"Those are your children." At the time of this event, we did not have children and were completely unable to conceive.

"My children?" I asked.

"Yes, I AM has many new things in store for you."

Needless to say, when Jonathan shared that with me, my soul was filled with the love of God. It reminded me of His great faithfulness. He is still the

Creator that creates out of no ing. He speaks into situations that are not yet, as though they are. It's ou job to walk out the truth He gives to us.

"Come on, I have more fo you to see," Jonathan said.

"More? But I have seen so much. Where are you taking me now?"

"There!!" Jonathan peere off to the distance and pointed towards the Throne.

My knees buckled, I was s nervous. I felt unworthy and unfit, yet somehow destined to go. I know Jo athan just said I was His son, but what about all the mistakes I've made, an how weak I feel at times? I am nobody and not from anywhere special.

"I AM knows all your inw d thoughts and has called you to come. You must go," Jonathan said.

We stepped into the char and off we went. The chariot seemed to be flying much higher in the air t s time. We were so high, that as I gazed back, my house appeared to be a tin miniature house I could pick up with my fingers. Even at this height the r gnificence of His Throne was more then my eyes could absorb. He was the ulsating Source of all Light, so bright, intense, and blazing purity. Light cons idating into perfect, white, fierce, passionate, raw power. The closer we got, ie chariot began to shake and I could feel His awesome Presence. He is an u natched vortex of raw power, and it was overwhelmingly evident; all life, a existence is held together by Him. There is no debate; nothing exists apar rom Him. He is I AM!!

We arrived in what seeme to be only a minute, but I was not wearing a watch. As we descended, I sa my first real shape. There were stairs rising up into thick intense clouds.

"Jonathan, are those. . .?"

"Shhhhh, you have to go this part alone, but be very, very quiet." We landed and I stepped out. I lo ed back at Jonathan and he simply motioned me to go forward.

THE GATE: ETERNITY BECKONS

The stairs were shaped like stairs you would see outside a courthouse or government building. They went on and on in both directions, with no end in sight. I instinctively removed the sandals I was wearing and took my first step. The stairs were pure gold, inlaid with countless gems, and yet also pure white. Words were inscribed everywhere, but I did not know what they said. There were thick clouds moving all around, very dense and intense. I could only see a little way in front of me. I did not know how many steps I climbed, but I knew I was nearing the top. I heard voices all around, and yet awesome, powerful, silence.

As I reached what I believed to be the top, I looked to the right and left, to see if anyone else was there, and I instantly got lost in the vastness. I heard a noise like rushing wings coming from above me. The clouds were so thick, I could not make out what it was, then *voooooom!!* Right over my head rushed an angel with six wings, singing: "Holy, holy, holy is the Lord Almighty; the whole earth is full of His Glory." The angel flew right over my head and back up into the thick clouds disappearing from my sight as quickly as he had come into view.

Slowly and methodically, the clouds straight ahead of me slightly parted, and I saw the smallest glimpse of Him sitting enthroned in front of me. I fell on my face!! There was not a thought, just pure reaction! His power was awesome and I knew no unrighteousness could stand before Him. I felt broken by my humanity and overwhelmed by His unstoppable, unimaginable raw Presence.

The Holy Spirit quietly spoke to my heart, with absolute kindness, and said, "Arise, my son." I did my best to stand, but my legs were complete jello and I knew they could give out at any second. He is God Almighty, and I was distinctly aware of what a vapor my life truly is, and yet somehow I knew I was His child and should be here. His Power is only matched by His Grace for giving me the strength and permission to be there.

You may have said this in your life—I know I have heard others say it—"When I stand before God, I have so many questions to ask Him." You might have questions, but you won't be asking them. Just standing a moment in His unmatched Presence will answer all of them without Him or you saying a word. You will just know, He is!

He was seated on a white throne. I could see His hands, feet, and some of His body, but His face was totally covered by clouds. There were words carved on the right and left arms of the Throne. The Holy Spirit spoke to my heart and said, "On the right is written 'Righteousness' and on the left is written 'Justice.'" I knew this was where all injustices were forever settled. No one gets away with anything, and we will all stand before Him to answer for our lives.

The Holy Spirit reminded me of this scripture:

> *"Dark clouds surround Him. Righteousness and Justice are the foundation of His Throne."* —Psalm 97:2 NKJV

I was standing before I AM. The Word, the very center of Truth and Life. There was thunder, lightning, clouds, and many voices like rushing water, mixed with Supreme Power.

> *"And, behold, the glory of the God of Israel came from the way of the east: and His voice was like a noise of many waters: and the earth shone with His glory."* —Ezekiel 43:2 NKJV

> *"His feet were like burnished bronze, refined in a furnace, and His voice was like the roar of many waters."* —Revelation 1:15 ESV

There was light and lavender reflecting everywhere. Mighty angels, with many wings, flew over my head and around His Throne. I stood in awe and wonder and, without thinking, I laid back down on my face. Suddenly, I was lifted up in the air and all I could see was lavender clouds all around me. I was not sure where I was, but knew I was not far from His Throne. The wispy lavender clouds hovered about, and I felt as though they were holding me in place.

As I gazed into the clouds, a long, rectangular, wooden box appeared out of the clouds and floated in front of me. It was ancient-looking. Somehow I instinctively knew this box could open, but I did not know what was inside. Suddenly, I heard the Lord's voice quietly speaking to my soul. "This box contains the secrets I want to share with My children. My children are presenting their needs, and I love answering those, but that rarely draws them close to My heart. I desire My children to seek My face, set themselves apart, and have Me be their first love in every area of their lives. I am a Jealous God, and I do not desire to be a segment they visit sometimes when they have a need. I AM their life source and if they would seek My face, I would share deep mysteries with them."

Again, I was suddenly lifted up and this time I was set back in the chariot. I stood in the chariot silently and Jonathan had us flying back through Heaven right away. As I gazed back, the clouds parted and I could see the briefest outline of the side of His face. I just caught a glimpse of His cheek, jaw and beard. I was a great distance away at the time, and it was completely awe-inspiring. He is absolutely beautiful and worth every sacrifice and any cost. I would lay my life down in a minute, if it brought Him glory. He is due all praise, all glory, and every ounce of all of us. Selfishness, pride, control, and any fleshly way has no place before Him.

Jonathan had my arm now, and stars blurred passed us as we exited Heaven. Earth zoomed in, then buildings and cars, the church, my shaking body, and with that, I was back. I was back in my body and the service was over. People were mingling around and I could tell they were waiting for me to be awake. I had no words, I only laid there and soaked a little longer in His Goodness and Love. I was totally wiped out, with little to no strength remaining. I slowly sat up and as my spirit man and body slowly merged back together, I started to get a glimpse of all the people around me with astonished looks. I saw my wife first with the biggest grin on her face, then other faces came into view. I felt like everyone wanted some grand speech from me, but frankly, my mind had not caught up with my spirit man and all that had just happened. I felt like a half-blended man inside, with absolutely no idea how to put myself back together.

A few minutes went by, an[d] my thoughts started to gather as I was starting to feel put back together. An [a]rtist friend showed me a picture he sketched while I was down "dancing" o[n] the carpet. It was the same outline of God's face that I saw for the slightes[t] moment in Heaven! Without me asking the question, he answered it. "W[hi]le you were on the ground shaking, your fingers mashed the carpet down [an]d I saw the image that I just showed you, so I thought I should sketch it." [Y]ou read that right, my spirit man in Heaven, my Earthly body shaking, my [fin]gers matting the image of His face in the carpet, and an artist to attest to i[t a]ll. Only God, who moves beyond our imagination, could demonstrate H[im]self that way!

Pop!!!

I am not sure if that is you[r] mind exploding or my mind reliving the story; let's call it even and just say b[oth] got blown.

My life was never the sa[me] after that day. Since then, I have been to Heaven many, many, many ti[m]es. In the following chapters I am going to take you on some of those adv[en]tures, and share all that I saw.

> *"The Lord rules! Let the earth rejoice! Let all the islands celebrate! Clouds and thick darkness surround God. His Throne is built on Righteousness and Justice. Fire proceeds before Him, burning up His enemies on every side. His lightning lights up the world; the earth sees it and trembles. The mountains melt like wax before the Lord, before the Lord of the whole world! Heaven has proclaimed God's Righteousness, and all nations have seen His glory. All those who worship images, those who are proud of idols, are put to shame. All gods bow down to the Lord! Zion has heard and celebrates, the towns of Judah rejoice because of Your acts of justice, Lord, because You, Lord, are the Most high over all the earth, because You are so superior to all other gods. Those of you who love the Lord, hate evil! God guards the lives of His faithful ones, delivering them from the power of the wicked. Light is planted like seeds for the righteous person; joy too for those whose heart is right. Rejoice in the Lord, righteous ones! Give thanks to His holy name!"* —Psalm 97 CEB

The Gate: Eternity Beckons

"The secret of the Lord is with those who fear Him, and He will show them His covenant." —Psalm 25:14 NKJV

CH APTER 6

ALL THI IGS BALANCED

I hope you are enjoying th book so far, because I am enjoying telling you about how great He is! It had een a few years since my debut on "Dancing with the Carpet." God has ta n me to Heaven many times now. I can't say I got used to it. How could I t's outside time and space, and each day, just like you, I sleep, eat, and live n Earth. I am a normal guy living a normal life, having very "abnormal" e eriences. That's why I'm writing this book, so I can tell people about ther

I would see angels on such regular basis that sometimes they just seemed like part of the family. I neve acked reverence at any point, but I was defi- nitely comfortable with the w the Holy Spirit chose to move. I had grown a ton from where I first start . I was not crippled by fear and insecurities anymore, and my confidence ew more and more each day in how amazing He is. No more hiding unde the sheet for me. The days of torment were long gone now.

We can get comfortable i knowing God and walking daily with Him, but let us never lose our holy ar of Him. That's not the kind of fear that makes us afraid of Him, it is t kind of fear that gives Him the reverence He so deserves. Let's make sure w nonor Him in the little things no one else sees so He can bless us with the bi hings. Deal? Good. "Fist pump was just ad- ministered."

Everything I'd seen in Heaven was so fun! Houses on top of water, built into mountains, in open prairies, by sandy beaches, and all somewhat recognizable, yet totally unique to Heaven, and built with things not of this world. Jesus is preparing some amazing places, so be about the Kingdom and He will be about your rewards. Wood, hay, and stubble. . .who wants that, go for the gems!

Many people can come to know the Lord, but if no one steps up to teach them how to walk in the Way, how are they going to know? God wants us to disciple others. Discipleship has always been a passion of mine and sadly, it is sorely lacking in so many places. I have never really understood why it lacks so much in so many places, because Jesus was so clear.

"Therefore go and make disciples of all nations, baptizing them in the name of the Father and of the Son and of the Holy Spirit." —Matthew 28:19 NLT

It's so important and can be so easy. Let me give you an example. Before I got married, I was leading a Bible Study on a secular college campus. We had about 50 people coming regularly, and we were continuing to grow weekly. I was busy preparing weekly messages and sometimes felt stressed about making sure each meeting went really smooth and just right. The Holy Spirit convicted me about it straight up, and told me to always focus on the relationship with people, not the function. He went on to tell me that function and program are not why Jesus hung on the Cross; the hearts and souls of people are. That message hit me hard and was so convicting. I saw in my own heart how easy it can be to find identity in what we do instead of Who we represent.

If you can grab hold of that shift it will change you, and open Eternal things over your life in a brand new way.

So I decided to stop stressing and started focusing on seeing each person who walked through the doors. One day, I saw a new man walk into the meeting. I noticed none of the leaders greeted him and you could tell right away he was nervous and feeling awkward. The meeting was about to start, but

again the Holy Spirit reminde⟨ ⟩ne of what He said and what to focus on. So,
I put my lesson down and wal⟨ ⟩d over to greet him. That simple act of kindness impacted him bigtime. ⟨ ⟩e chatted for a few minutes and I found out
his name, and a little about hir⟨ ⟩ As our brief conversation went on, his shoulders relaxed and he came in ar⟨ ⟩took a seat. Not everyone believes church is
a safe place, but that day he f⟨ ⟩safe in this place. . .

I learned many years later⟨ ⟩hat he debated staying if no one was going to
be friendly—and at that time⟨ ⟩e did not know about Jesus. What a sad day,
if we fail to show simple love⟨ ⟩nd value to a lost person who so desperately
needs it. I hung out with th⟨ ⟩man often, always doing simple things that
were fun. One day he gave h⟨ ⟩life to Christ, and I was able to take time to
teach him the simple truth ab⟨ ⟩t Who God is. He went on to be a great hus-
band, father, and a firefighter.⟨ ⟩Iis faith is so strong and his life has impacted
so many in incredible ways. ⟨ ⟩hat if that hello was not given? Discipleship
can start that simply.

Now, honestly, sometime⟨ ⟩liscipleship can be really hard. It can require
forbearance and longsuffering⟨ ⟩ut that doesn't change the fact that Jesus said
to do it. I ran into one of tho⟨ ⟩really difficult ones as I was trying to disciple
a man who was living a very d⟨ ⟩ructive life and deeply damaging his marriage
and family. He claimed to be⟨ ⟩believer, but continually failed to listen to instruction. He continually cho⟨ ⟩e his own will over the Will and Word of the
Lord. That is not a good rec⟨ ⟩e for blessing or success. God's Word is the
standard and we will all be he⟨ ⟩to that standard when we stand before Him
one day. This man's constant r⟨ ⟩ellion troubled my heart deeply and I needed
to know how these continued⟨ ⟩noices were reverberating in Eternity. I asked
The Lord to open my eyes to⟨ ⟩ternity and help me see things from His perspective.

A few nights later as I⟨ ⟩vas laying down in my bed, suddenly. . .
Zooooooooom!! Out of my body⟨ ⟩nd straight to the Pearly Gate. I had no time
to dance on this one, and ho⟨ ⟩stly the whole speed of it really jarred me. I
felt a bit nervous, because thi⟨ ⟩time no angel escorted me to Heaven, I just

popped out of my body and popped straight to the Gate. I was definitely feeling out of sorts and a bit tentative as to why I was there.

I hear your question already: "Why would God move that way, knowing it would make me uncomfortable?" I, like you, need the Holy Spirit's daily discipleship and sometimes that comes in the form of messing with my comfort level. It drives my dependance on Him.

I stood in front of the Pearly Gate, and as it slowly opened, Jonathan, the angel, stepped towards me. "Nice of you to come."

"Thanks, but I didn't really feel I had a choice," I said.

"You always have a choice. Making room for the Lord's Spirit and allowing the Lord to pull you out of your body is a choice of surrender."

"I never thought about it that way."

Jonathan looked at me and smiled, "Surrender is always a choice."

As I stepped through the Pearly Gate, Heaven's glory overwhelmed me. It's impossible to get used to seeing His glory permeate everything. Heaven is so alive and active, life and brilliance flowing everywhere. Picture yourself standing on the coastline of Norway, staring out into the ocean with rocks jutting out all over. Go ahead and look it up, so you have a picture in your mind. Now, count every ripple of water, every snowflake on the distant mountains, every flower blowing in the wind. Got them all? That's 1/1,000,000th of what your senses experience in the first 10 seconds through the Gate. This world is not worth your focus, but His Kingdom sure is!

Way off in the distance it looked as though 10,000 suns had collided with 10,000 suns, in one spot combining their brilliant light. It was so good to see the Throne again, even if it was a great distance away. The colors, the brilliance, the peace, the beauty, His presence, were all simply magnificent, except for this one thing.

I gazed to the left, and standing there by the Gate was a man dressed in a dingy gray tunic. I watched as he bent down and started to tenderly and methodically touch and speak to one flower. What he said and what exactly he was doing I did not know. It was very clear though, he took this very, very seriously. He was supremely focused on the single flower. He then moved to the next flower and went through a very similar routine. Heaven is populated with billions, if not trillions of flowers. There are mountains, valleys, rivers, lakes, and also many things that are not on Earth. In this particular place, where this dingy dressed man was standing, there were only four flowers. Why only four and why is he the only one interested in them? I did not know. There was no one else around anywhere, except me and Jonathan. The man didn't seem to notice us there or at least pay us any mind. Even though the gray tunic stood starkly out against the backdrop of mind blowing, vibrant colors, there was a quiet joy and peace to him in all he did. . . I had to know more.

"Jonathan, what is that man doing?"

"He is tending what The Lord has given Him."

"I don't understand. There are only four flowers and nothing else around."

"While on Earth this man did not listen to instruction or the Word of The Lord. Though he truly accepted Jesus as his Savior, he chose not to listen to the instructions he was given. His choices caused great damage to those around him. Though his salvation was secure in Jesus alone, without works, his disobedience reaped no rewards in Heaven."

"Wow, Jonathan, that is so !"

"Yes it is. The Lord's Word is true. Whatever a people sow they will reap and people need to be about storing treasures in Heaven. By the way, you know this man."

"What? Who is he?" I said

Just then the man turned slightly and I did know him. It was the man from Earth I was trying to disciple. I did not speak to him, but suddenly the Holy Spirit birthed revelation in my heart. This man has a wife and three kids on Earth. A question burst within me. "Jonathan, do the four flowers represent his family?"

"Yes they do. He did not tend to them on Earth properly so this is his assignment in Eternity. Each person the Lord gives you to intimately love is very, very serious to Him. Your actions on Earth always reverberate in Eternity. Your choices regarding the assignments the Lord gives you, shape what rewards are waiting for you in Eternity. Obedience really does matter. Honor and obey the Lord on Earth and great rewards await you in Eternity. Dishonor the Lord and continually choose disobedience and no rewards will be awaiting you."

"Why the dingy gray tunic?"

"In eternity he stands far from the Glory of the Lord on His Throne, and that is why his tunic appears dingy gray. Even so, the glory of the Lord on that man would light up the darkest corridor of Hell."

"Jonathan, Heaven is so amazing. I want all the Lord has for me."

"The Lord's Grace is always there and always available. Man will fail, but walking in a state of a surrendered heart towards Him opens up the greatness of Heaven and stores up treasures impossible to imagine, that you get to enjoy for all of Eternity. Remember what Jesus said in the book of Revelation to the seven churches and how He expects them to live. Jesus' words are Eternal and as humans, it's vital you understand the weight of them."

> "Write this letter to the angel of the church in Sardis. This is the message from the One who has the sevenfold Spirit of God and the seven stars: I know all the things you do, and that you have a reputation for being alive—but you are dead. Wake up! Strengthen what little remains, for even what is left is almost dead. I find that your actions do not meet the requirements of my God. Go back to what you heard and believed at first; hold to it firmly. Repent and turn to me again. If you don't wake up, I will come to you suddenly, as unexpected as a thief. Yet there are some in the church in Sardis who have not soiled their clothes with evil. They

will walk with me in w te, for they are worthy. All who are victorious will be clothed white. I will never erase their names from the Book of Life, l t I will announce before my Father and his angels that they are r ne. Anyone with ears to hear must listen to the Spirit and under and what he is saying to the churches."
—Revelation 3:1–6 NI

"Why are all those people tanding in a line over there?"

"I am glad you asked. Le take a look."

The line was long, *really* ong. Being outside of time and space, who knows what the distance was, ut to my appearance it was miles. I'll never complain about a line at the ocery store again! The line wound to a lake that looked very much like the incoln Memorial Reflecting Pool. It was surrounded by massive trees that d huge fruit hanging from them. A river fed into the lake that appeared to nd its way toward the Throne. It was a place filled with joy and peace. I c ld tell everyone had a genuine excitement in what they were doing. As I sto d there and watched, people would walk over, grab some fruit and take a bit

"All of these people you s are similar to the man in the dingy tunic." Jonathan said. "While on Ea , they walked in different levels of disobedience and are now unable to ac ss the deeper parts of Glory the Lord had prepared for them. They need to t the fruit to give them strength to get closer to the Throne. There are realn of Glory that God has waiting for His people, but only obedience opens the up over their life. Many of these choices of obedience may bring sufferin but suffering draws you closer to the Savior, and opens up deeper realms of lory in Eternity. The Lord loves all, but there are no shortcuts to intimacy w h Him. If He said it through the Word, then that is the standard all are hel o."

I could see that each bite fused people with a deeper sense of joy and excitement. This was not a t ious or foreboding task. The Lord spoke to my heart and said, "Faith is th gateway, so once you pass into Eternity, then faith does not have the same f ction as it did on Earth. I will not compromise Who I AM, My Word, or My Holiness. People must take Me seriously when I speak. These people, just like everyone else in Heaven, were saved through faith in My finished work on the Cross alone, without works. Works do not save you in any way, only the finished work of the Cross does. The Cross is the starting point to walking out a life with Me. I desire that My children move from milk to meat and chase the deeper Truths of Who I AM. If My children have a foot in the world and a mind of the world, then they will not know My Will for them and will miss out. Remember what it says in the book of Romans."

> *"And so, dear brothers and sisters, I plead with you to give your bodies to God because of all he has done for you. Let them be a living and holy sacrifice—the kind he will find acceptable. This is truly the way to worship him. Don't copy the behavior and customs of this world, but let God transform you into a new person by changing the way you think. Then you will learn to know God's will for you, which is good and pleasing and perfect."* —Romans 12:1–2 NLT

As I stood there, a very kind-faced man approached me. "Hi, my name is Jerry."

"Hi Jerry, I am Scott."

God's radiance beamed off his face and colors reflected and refracted from him all over the place. It was amazing to see! Without my saying a word, he began to share. "I was a pastor on Earth and I loved the Lord, but too many of my motives were selfish. I had such great head knowledge of Him, but my heart failed to grab the relationship He so desires. I did good works, shared His name, but I failed to understand He wanted my heart above all things." With that, Jerry returned to his friends and I stood there soaking in all I had heard. The word "obedience" pulsated through my soul.

I am not sure how much longer I stood in Heaven that day, but it seemed like a very long time. I soaked in all I could see. I had a somberness in my heart to be diligent to walk with God from my heart and not just my head.

Suddenly, I was back in my body and I laid awake pondering all the Lord had revealed.

Even though I lived the events of this book, as I retell these stories, it has caused me to reflect even deeper. My hope is that this book is encouraging you and challenging you to go deeper with Him and reflect on all He has done for us.

> *"Let him who is taught the word share in all good things with him who teaches. Do not be deceived, God is not mocked; for whatever a man sows, that he will also reap. For he who sows to his flesh will of the flesh reap corruption, but he who sows to the Spirit will of the Spirit reap everlasting life. And let us not grow weary while doing good, for in due season we shall reap if we do not lose heart. Therefore, as we have opportunity, let us do good to all, especially to those who are of the household of faith."* —Galatians 6:6–10 NKJV

> *"Do not lay up for yourselves treasures on earth, where moth and rust destroy and where thieves break in and steal; but lay up for yourselves treasures in heaven, where neither moth nor rust destroys and where thieves do not break in and steal. For where your treasure is, there your heart will be also."* —Matthew 6:19–21 NKJV

The Gate: Eternity Beckons

CHAPTER 7

THE GREAT PHYSICIAN

Illness can strike us all. Sometimes there is understanding and sometimes there is not. I know God is a healer because I have seen Him heal over and over again. With that being said, I have struggled with doubts and fears along the way. Sickness has hit my home hard at times, but God has brought incredible testimony out of it too. We do have an enemy of our souls, that wants nothing less than our total destruction. Our enemy will use anything he can get his hands on to steal, kill, and destroy us, but one day he will face his ultimate destruction. What a great day that will be!

If I have learned anything in going to Heaven, it is that God is a good God. His goodness and love permeate every aspect of Heaven. I felt His goodness many times, but in Heaven it is like the air you breath. His goodness saturates you and flows through your being. After visiting Heaven so many times, the starkness of coming back to Earth has gotten harder and harder. Earth is beautiful, but compared to Heaven, its beauty is like looking at an old weathered postcard of a pretty resort in a distant land. Compare the weathered postcard to the most beautiful resort known to man and multiply it by a billion, to get the smallest of comparisons. The Fall and sin has had their effect on Earth, but it has no influence or place in Heaven. Oh,what a place He has in store for you and me! Put your Eternally minded hat on daily and point the rudder of your heart towards His Kingdom. Build your treasure there, not here.

THE GATE: ETERNITY BECKONS

Because we live in a fallen world and so far from His perfection, not everything on this side of Heaven will be understood. In my journeys to Heaven, I have definitely learned that God is so far beyond our ability to comprehend. He has no end, and seeking Him with all we have is so incredible and worth every minute spent. I hope you are starting to see that too. He is also God, and it is important that no matter what our trials are, we see Him as both loving and compassionate, but also as God Almighty. Because He is God Almighty, we will not understand all His ways, but He is always good. It is always important to be about His business and not our own agenda so we can enjoy the fullness of His great promises in His Word.

> *"And the Holy Spirit helps us in our weakness. For example, we don't know what God wants us to pray for. But the Holy Spirit prays for us with groanings that cannot be expressed in words. And the Father who knows all hearts knows what the Spirit is saying, for the Spirit pleads for us believers in harmony with God's own will. And we know that God causes everything to work together for the good of those who love God and are called according to his purpose for them."* —Romans 8:26–28

I was in my bedroom one evening, settling down for the night. I had just watched my football team win and I had had a great dinner to go along with it. Are you a foodie? I sure can be. I find myself cooking a meal, imagining what my next meal will be. Pastries are my weakness and a good bakery can break me. Haha! Those warm smells bring weakness to my knees. Sorry, food distracts me, back on point.

As I was saying, we live in a fallen world—and my wife and I were facing some real trials in this season of our lives. We were at a crossroads of a promise God had given us for children and our inability to conceive. We had only been married a few years and sickness had struck my wife's body and she fell very ill. Doctors could not diagnose her condition and we were running out of earthly answers. I was heartbroken over all of it. As I shared earlier, being married was top of my list, and she was the love of my life. How could we be going through this? After all the trials leading up to marriage, why was the thought of losing her in front of me on a daily basis? Those questions and many others raced through my mind as we battled this illness.

It's easy to have our emotions override our spiritual senses. We are human, but we are spiritual people only passing through this world to our Eternal destination. Pain is real, loss is real, but never lose hope in how good He really is and how deeply He loves you. As I was saying before, this particular night I watched some football, had a nice dinner and was off to bed. None of the trials we were facing were on my mind this particular night, but they were on His.

I layed down and the Holy Spirit's Presence fell in the room. Suddenly, as my mind drifted onto Him, my body began to shake violently, then pop, out of my body I jumped. I would love to tell you by now my "dancing" had gotten much more dignified, but nothing could be farther from the truth. I looked like a fish out of water, flopping to get back in. I often told my wife, you didn't marry me for my graceful elegance. Haha! Jonathan (the angel), was right there. As usual, he had a smile stretching ear to ear and kindness emanated from his face. He grabbed my arm and off to Heaven we went. We entered through the beautiful Gate of pearl and sped with lightning speed through Heaven.

Jonathan was not saying anything, so I asked, "Why so quiet?" Jonathan simply replied, "Shhhh, just look." As the scene came into view, I saw two massive buildings. Their proportions were overwhelming. They sat behind another gate and over that gate it read: "Fashioning Place." Jonathan dropped me off at the Fashioning Place gate and motioned for me to go in. As I entered, I was overwhelmed by the scale of these buildings. The building on the left had these words written on it, "Needs to be met." The building on the right had the words written on it, "Those to come." A very friendly angel started walking towards me with a huge smile on his face. He was wearing a lab coat and was about my height. I am a 6 8 man masquerading in a 5 8 man's body, in case you were curious. In other words, though I wish I were tall, I definitely am not.

"Come, we've been expecting you. Let me show you inside," the angel spoke. I was totally speechless and just in awe. There were more angels than I could count, flying all over the place. I have to admit, angels are just spectacular. I love seeing their joy, excitement, and fun personalities. They are all uniquely made, and designed for His purposes. Considering one angel wiped out 185,000 men in an evil army, their power is pretty incredible. Read 2 Kings 19 for the reference. Angels truly are amazing to see, yet not as amazing to see the look in a person's eyes who first understands Jesus' great love for them. Jesus hung on the Cross for us, not for angels.

Back to our story. First, the angel led me to the building that read, "Needs to be met." As the door opened, I was again overwhelmed by the sheer size. Everywhere, in very orderly fashion there were human body parts. Nothing gory or in anyway disturbing. It was beautiful. Legs were with legs, arms with arms, hands with hands, and so on. Every part of our human bodies, that God has made, were there. Some were on racks, some in drawers, and they were all different sizes, shapes, and colors; very organized and tenderly watched over. The angel saw the questions in my eyes, and without me saying a word, he spoke; "This place is a storehouse for all the healings that I AM wants to release. We tend this continually, until the prayers of the saints reach His Throne. Come, come, let me show you more."

We left that building and proceeded over to the building with the words written; "Those to come." As we walked through the door, I could tell the scale was great, but somehow the inside of this place felt much more intimate. There was sweet, sweet lullaby music being played throughout. It was so quiet and so peaceful. Nothing like the other building that had a distinct hustle to it. It was dark, but had sparkling lights all around. I saw what appeared to be gray and silver, twinkling stars everywhere, suspending in the silky, smooth darkness. Off to the right I saw angels standing in what appeared to be windows. They had such a look of excitement on their face and they were standing in a posture that looked like they were ready to launch. The angel in the lab coat spoke, "They are delivering souls to the womb they will grow in. They get so excited to be a part of who the Great I AM is creating." Angels were exploding off the window sills in incredible light displays, bringing their packages to Earth. The angel in the lab coat came over to me and motioned for me to climb a set of stairs that led to the window sills. I am not sure how high or long they were. They seemed to move in a spiral formation and I'm happy to note, I was not winded when I got to the top. All those pastries have not gotten me yet!

The windows went on in a perfect straight line as far as my eyes could see. "Come on, time for a ride," the angel in the lab coat said. He motioned for me to walk over to an angel standing in one of the window sills. As I walked over, the angel grabbed me tight and exploded off the window sill! We started flying back towards Earth with a blaze of speed.

I knew we were in the United States somewhere, and I was standing in a hallway of an apartment building. It was a simple, plain hallway with doors lining both sides. The angel had something in his hand, but I could not make it out. He motioned for me to stay there as he passed through the door. Yes, I was still out of my body, but fully aware. I could not see through any walls and when the angel motioned for me to stay, I simply did. He came back with the biggest smile, joy exploded from his face. "Okay, mission accomplished. Package is delivered. The Creator is so fun!"

With that he grabbed me tight again, and we exploded back from Earth straight to the building called, "Those to Come." As soon as the angel landed, other angels gathered around to give him high fives and listen to where he delivered his package. As I stood there, another angel motioned with his finger to come over to him. As I walked over, he grabbed me tight and again we exploded into the air and back to Earth in a streak of brilliant light! This time I knew I was in an African village. We landed in the middle of the village next to a closed hut. This angel did what the last angel did and motioned for me to stay there as he passed through the outer wall of the hut. He had something in his hand too that I could not make out. This time the angel came out dancing, joy again exploding from his face, and smiling from ear to ear.

"Let's go!" he said. Quick grab, and we were blasting back towards Heaven. We landed right back at the same window sill from which we left. Once again another angel motioned me over to their window. It was a female angel and shorter than me. Height really doesn't matter, because this gal could move. When she grabbed me and shot off the window sill, I felt like I was going faster than I was with the other two angels.

This time we were in the inner city of an Asian country. In the spirit you know things that your mind would be way too slow to figure out. We were at the front door of a home, and just like before, she motioned for me to wait outside. Once again, she held an object in her hand, but just like the other two times, I could not make out what it was. She passed through the door and, within moments of entering, she came out beaming with joy. "Oh, how many are the Creator's thoughts towards those He has made," she said. She quietly walked over and motioned for me to stand by her side, as if I knew what was coming and should be well versed. Boom! Right off the street, stars streaking past, and back on her window sill.

This time I stood for a bit of time and just looked down, soaking in the incredible place where I was standing. Every time an angel would blast off the window, the other angels would shout for joy, "The Lord just created another one!" It was quite the party atmosphere on this side of the building. It was incredible to see all the light and colors of angels exploding from window sills up against this silky, gentle, black silhouette. Watching the beautiful little white lights suspended in this silky "nothingness" was extraordinary to watch. The mix of gentleness and joy was so fun to experience.

I closed my eyes and soaked up the peace of the building, and then suddenly I was back in my body.

"If you will listen carefully to the voice of the Lord your God and do what is right in His sight, obeying His commands and keeping all His decrees, then I will not make you suffer any of the diseases I sent on the Egyptians; for I am the Lord who heals you." —Exodus 15:26 NLT

"Bless the Lord, O my soul, and all that is within me, bless His holy name! Bless the Lord, O my soul, and forget not all His benefits, Who forgives all your iniquities, Who heals all your diseases, Who redeems your life from the pit, Who crowns you with steadfast love

and mercy, Who satisfies you with good so that your youth is renewed like the eagle's. The Lord works righteousness and justice for all who are oppressed." —Psalm 103:1–6 ESV

"And great crowds came to him, bringing with them the lame, the blind, the crippled, the mute, and many others, and they put them at his feet, and he healed them." —Matthew 15:30 ESV

"That evening they brought to Him many who were oppressed by demons, and He cast out the spirits with a word and healed all who were sick." —Matthew 8:16 ESV

"Is anyone among you sick? Let him call for the elders of the church, and let them pray over him, anointing him with oil in the name of the Lord. And the prayer of faith will save the one who is sick, and the Lord will raise him up." —James 5:14–15 ESV

"You made all the delicate, inner parts of my body and knit me together in my mother's womb. Thank you for making me so wonderfully complex! Your workmanship is marvelous—how well I know it. You watched me as I was being formed in utter seclusion, as I was woven together in the dark of the womb. You saw me before I was born. Every day of my life was recorded in your book. Every moment was laid out before a single day had passed. How precious are your thoughts about me, O God. They cannot be numbered! I can't even count them; they outnumber the grains of sand! And when I wake up, you are still with me!" —Psalms 139:13–16 NLT

CHAPTER 8

THE WAIT IS WORTH IT

Seeing the "Needs to be met" and "Those to come" at the "Fashioning Place" was amazing! Time had gone on since visiting the "Fashioning Place" and my wife was still very ill, and I was still seeking answers. Her body was breaking, and because of the undiagnosed issues, it caused her reproductive organs to stop working. We deeply wanted children and believed God would give them to us, but this battle was real and we had to guard against losing hope. The chances of having children in the natural was not looking good on any level, let alone my wife being well again. Although the news of illness struck us hard, our faith did not waver and we would not back off His promise to us.

One particular day I was at work and having a conversation with God about all of this. I was outside at the time, and suddenly I saw a figure approaching. It was an angel. He had a sword hanging in a sheath, a golden belt, wearing a tunic, walking in sandals, and golden light emanating from his being. You know, all the standard angel stuff. Haha! As he walked towards me he had something in his hand. He put his hand out, palm up to show me what he was holding. In his hand sat a clear glass box no bigger than his palm. In the glass box was a gray, silver, and white twinkling star. That's the best way I can describe it. "This is the soul of your child to come." With that, he closed his palm, placed the box inside a pouch on his belt, and flew off. It completely stunned me! Of course, I called my wife right away and shared with her the great news! She received it with faith and excitement.

THE GATE: ETERNITY BECKONS

Years passed by, and my wife's health slowly improved. She was still not whole and we could not conceive. I had been to Heaven many times more and I often thought of the angel that held the box with my child's soul inside, yet each day we walked with no answer to our infertility. Many other people we knew, both friends and family had multiple children, with no struggles to conceive. We did not lose faith, but we did have many nights filled with tears. The pain of the wait was real. The pain of my wife's illness was real.

The biggest way the enemy of our souls tried to sneak in was through a root of bitterness. The enemy would often tempt us to turn away from God and question His love for us. Don't ever give into that; bitterness is a killer. We didn't give in either. Bitterness is complete rottenness to our souls and a stealer of our joy.

In the midst of all this struggle, God gave me a powerful dream. A really long, super-detailed, life-shaping dream. I would love to take the time to tell you all about it here, but I'll cover that in a future book so we can stay on topic. In part of the dream I saw my wife fully pregnant and dressed in all black. She had just climbed to the top of a mountain and stood there totally at peace. In the dream she was content and in life she was just the same. Before any of these struggles with illness and infertility came, my wife was given the gift of Faith. That gift, and its demonstrated power through peace and contentment, was incredible to watch. Nothing rattled her and nothing, no matter how grave the news or deep the hurt, diminished her Faith in the One that held all power. I was so proud of her faith and her reckless abandon in Jesus. She completely trusted in His ability to carry her through anything, no matter what the results were.

More time went by. It had now been 13 years in total since I saw the angel with the box. Thirteen years of daily walking out unanswered prayers. Thirteen years of fending off discouragement and desires to give up. I really want you to let the 13 years sink in for a minute. God is outside of time, even though He speaks into our time-filled and constrained lives.

During that time the Lord called us to move across the country. Like usual, we went with little instruction, but clearly hearing from Him. We were in a definite place of major transition and new beginnings. My wife's health had improved, but I started noticing that her body seemed off again. She went to the doctor and sure enough some things were unbalanced. We had gone through this for so many years, this was nothing unusual.

A few days after that appointment, we were in the midst of moving and I was working hard unloading a moving truck for our new place. As I unloaded my last box, I walked into our bedroom totally exhausted from moving day. Sweat poured down my brow, and all I wanted to do was sit, recline in my favorite chair, and eat a sandwich. My wife walked into the bedroom grinning ear to ear. I figured she was admiring my busting biceps, so I sucked the belly in and stood a little taller. She didn't even notice them and quietly handed me a bag. I panicked inside! Housewarming gifts? I didn't know we were getting each other housewarming gifts! We had never done that before. Out of the bag I pulled out a baby's bib, then I pulled out a book entitled, "I Love You, Daddy." Grinning ear to ear, my wife saw the shock on my face, and just looked back at me, smiling away. I asked if it was true, and with tears streaming down both of our faces, my wife just nodded her head and mouthed the word yes. One day I will publically share the video with all of you, showing that day. Needless to say I was in total shock and it took a solid three days for my brain to catch up with what my spirit man knew to be true. We were pregnant!

For all those 13 years of waiting, we always believed God was giving us a boy. Even had a name picked out for him. We went to the ultrasound only to discover a beautiful little girl, hand delivered by an angel, straight from "Those to come," almost four months prior. God totally concealed her for all those years, and all those weeks. We had totally missed my wife's first trimester and had no idea we were pregnant! That is why I had the dream and saw my wife in black. God was concealing this great work He was doing.

Up to this point, other than my wife, I had never told anyone about the angel I met outside with my child's soul. The Holy Spirit was very clear that I was not allowed to share it, so I carried it close to my heart. When the climb became the hardest, we would often talk about it.

During the pregnancy, some great gals got together and threw a baby shower for my wife. They played games, laughed, ate, and had a great time. My wife opened the gifts and saw that someone bought a beautiful baby's bassinet as a gift. It was white, but something was distinctly on the mattress. All over the mattress was gray and silver starbursts! That's right, you got it, just like what the angel showed me. Just like it looked in the "Those to come" building in Heaven. We wept, and for the first time I started to share the story of what God had shown 13 years earlier. God had given His "yes" 13 years earlier, but He built a testimony to share with all of you. The pain of carrying this and waiting was real, but so was His answer. The pregnancy went great, no issues, and five months later I was able to look my baby girl in the eyes. I had met her years earlier, but didn't know it, twinkling away in Heaven waiting to be delivered.

"I wait for the Lord, my soul waits, and in His word I do hope."
—Psalms 130:5 ESV

"Uphold my steps in Your paths, That my footsteps may not slip. I have called upon You, for You will hear me, O God; Incline Your ear to me, and hear my speech." —Psalms 17:5–6 NKJV

"May He grant you according to your heart's desire, And fulfill all your purpose. We will rejoice in your salvation, And in the name of our God we will set up our banners! May the Lord fulfill all your petitions. Now I know that the Lord saves His anointed; He will answer him from His holy heaven with the saving strength of His right hand." —Psalms 20:4–6 NKJV

"Bend down, O Lord, and hear my prayer; answer me, for I need Your help. Protect me, for I am devoted to You. Save me, for I serve You and trust You. You are my God. Be merciful to me, O Lord, for I am calling on You constantly. Give me happiness, O Lord, for I give myself to You. O Lord, You are so good, so ready to forgive, so full of unfailing love for all who ask for Your help. Listen closely to

my prayer, O Lord; hear my urgent cry. I will call to You whenever I'm in trouble, and You will answer me." —Psalms 86:1–7 NLT

THE GATE: ETERNITY BECKONS

CHAPTER 9

ASK, SEEK, KNOCK:
YOUR ANSWERS ARE COMING

God holds the whole universe together. He is all-powerful and unmatched in His glory and strength. He is our only Hope and our only Way. If you and I are anything alike, it is easy to get discouraged by unanswered prayers. It's all too easy to doubt, and turn away to find our answers in other places. God's delays or unanswered prayers are not a lack of love or care, but His desire for our desperation. All too often we forget that God is outside of time and space, but He has compassion for us in our frail state.

> *"The Lord is like a father to His children, tender and compassionate to those who fear Him. For He knows how weak we are; He remembers we are only dust. Our days on earth are like grass; like wildflowers, we bloom and die. The wind blows, and we are gone— as though we had never been here. But the love of the Lord remains forever with those who fear Him." —Psalms 103:13–17 NLT*

Persistence is everything when seeking the Lord for answers. I have learned more and thanked Him the most for all the nos I received, before I received the yes. Nos may bring disappointment and sometimes that disappointment can really hurt. Trust me, I totally understand. Really! Many nos I've received have brought brokenness and tears. It is so important that in all the nos we always thank God, and even ask Him for strength to continue to believe in His goodness. It's hard sometimes, really hard, but don't allow emotions to dictate the Joy and Peace He has for you in all situations.

At this point, I definitely enjoyed traveling to Heaven. Now that I write that it sounds funny. Of course, I enjoyed traveling to Heaven! How could I not? It's Heaven! Haha! As I said before, the more and more I was taken, the harder and harder it became to come back to Earth. Heaven is our home and at times that call to be there was so overwhelming; I did not want to leave. I ached so deeply to stay. Being there is contentment, peace, rest, and belonging. The influence of the fallen world does not exist and the thought of that alone was so, so good. I knew though that God had a plan for my life and that I had people on Earth who needed me. That was the one thing that made coming back easier. The more often I went to Heaven, the longer it would take me to adjust to life back on Earth. How long and intense the trip was definitely had a direct correlation for how long it took me to adjust back to life as I knew it. Sometimes it would only take a few hours, other times a few days, sometimes a few weeks. No matter how long it took to adjust, the tension of how to walk out day-to-day life, with the growing knowledge of Heaven, was getting difficult.

Not to mention, I saw in the spirit every day. Sometimes demons and the different activities of the kingdom of darkness. Other times I would see wars in the heavens when territory was being taken. I would see angels all the time too, in different capacities. I never fully had the answer on how to balance it all, so I don't try anymore. At this time, I did not know if the Holy Spirit was going to give me a full answer to why I was experiencing these things. His only guidance most times was to surrender and share with others when the time was right. To keep momentum going, that's what I did. I have a strong analytical side and in order to not seize up by process, I simply obeyed and let it flow. I don't share everything I see all the time; that's where Wisdom and waiting on the Lord are absolutely key. We must wait on Him in all things and allow Him to guide our lips. Remember our tongues are like a rudder and can steer the course of our lives. Be careful what you speak and be careful of what you don't.

Ready for another trip?

Like other times before, I had laid my head down on my pillow, when Jonathan entered my room and off to Heaven we went. Every time he came, I always had to surrender and allow him to take me. Choice is never removed. We blasted through space, stars in total blurs of light, through the Gate, and into Heaven's sky. As we flew, off in the great distance, I saw I AM sitting on His Throne. Clouds surrounded Him, as power pulsated from His Being. Jonathan directed our flight path towards the Throne and my heart instantly began to flutter.

We were flying on His left side and once again, His face was covered, but I could see the Throne and an outline of His body. I would fail miserably here to try and describe the colors and sheer sense of absolute, immense power emanating from Him. He simply IS. All things are held together by Him and there is no one like Him. He is the Great I AM! I noticed something distinct, slightly offset behind Him. It stood out, because compared to all the light exploding off of Him, this was totally black. As we got closer it looked like a black mountain with tiny white lights all over it. It almost looked ash-like and I soon realized the white lights were angels. As we got closer, I noticed the angels were removing this "ash" substance from the mountain, putting it in golden bowls, and flying towards the Throne. I was very silent; I knew we were in a Holy place and speaking was not my best option. I actually started to learn not to blurt out the first thing that came to my mind, but instead, just listen and take it all in.

Jonathan, seeing questions all over my face, began to explain. "This is the mountain of incense where all the prayers of the saints come. Each prayer is tenderly cared for and put in a specific bowl depending on the need. Each need is then brought before the Throne." I watched as angels would go up into the Throne to present the prayers in their bowl to Him. The angels would leave the Throne, holding a scroll for the answer that I AM had given. Each angel would burst from the Throne with such a sense of honor and purpose. New angels continued to arrive, adding new prayers of incense. The mountain was continually alive with activity.

THE GATE: ETERNITY BECKONS

The angels bringing the "incense," tending the mountain, presenting the bowls, and leaving Heaven all looked distinctly different. I could tell by their different looks and clothes they wore, that each had a specific function. Some had swords, some had spears, some wore robes, while others were in full battle gear. Their colors and sense of purpose were something to behold. They were fully devoted to I AM and genuinely excited to minister to the saints. He really loves us and they love serving Him. I was reminded in Daniel when the angel is released to bring an answer, but the angel was at war for 21 days with the prince of darkness that was over that region.

Demons and demonic power are real. I don't just want this book to encourage you and get you excited for where you will be one day if you know Jesus. I also want this book to also challenge you to go deeper and grow in wisdom. Demons were once angels that resided in Heaven. They saw how Heaven worked and each had roles and functions there. They know that place that we on this side of the Gate access by faith. This is also what makes them such effective liars, because they are lying about a place they once called home. Jesus called Satan the father of lies. Satan and demon's native tongue is lying. They will twist any level of truth to hinder our ability to have a relationship with the Lord. This also makes it extremely important that we understand authority and dependency. We have no power on our own, but demons do. We do have power through what Jesus bought and won on the Cross. Start with His words on the subject and let Him teach you from there.

> *"When the seventy-two disciples returned, they joyfully reported to him, 'Lord, even the demons obey us when we use your name!' 'Yes,' he told them, 'I saw Satan fall from heaven like lightning! Look, I have given you authority over all the power of the enemy, and you can walk among snakes and scorpions and crush them. Nothing will injure you. But don't rejoice because evil spirits obey you; rejoice because your names are registered in heaven.'"*—Luke 10:17–20 NLT

> *"O Lord, I am calling to you. Please hurry! Listen when I cry to you for help! Accept my prayer as incense offered to you, and my upraised hands as an evening offering. Take control of what I say,*

O Lord, and guard my lips. Don't let me drift toward evil or take part in acts of wickedness. Don't let me share in the delicacies of those who do wrong." —Psalms 141:1–4 NLT

"Then another angel with a gold incense burner came and stood at the altar. And a great amount of incense was given to him to mix with the prayers of God's people as an offering on the gold altar before the Throne. The smoke of the incense, mixed with the prayers of God's holy people, ascended up to God from the altar where the angel had poured them out." —Revelation 8:3–4 NLT

"Keep on asking, and you will receive what you ask for. Keep on seeking, and you will find. Keep on knocking, and the door will be opened to you. For everyone who asks, receives. Everyone who seeks, finds. And to everyone who knocks, the door will be opened. You parents—if your children ask for a loaf of bread, do you give them a stone instead? Or if they ask for a fish, do you give them a snake? Of course not! So if you sinful people know how to give good gifts to your children, how much more will your heavenly Father give good gifts to those who ask Him." —Matthew 7:7–11 NLT

CHAPTER 10

THE ACCUSER

It had been a busy day of work, gardening, cooking dinner, and house chores. Nothing abnormal had happened this particular day. To be honest, Heaven had not been on my mind. Boy, did that change! I was finishing up a delicious bowl of cookie-dough ice cream, while doing my final cleanup of the kitchen dishes just before bed. I don't know about you, but I don't like cleaning dishes, so rewarding myself with a bowl of delicious creamy goodness only seemed right.

I finished cleaning up the kitchen and off to bed I went. I was super tired from the day and was deeply looking forward to letting my head crash the pillow and my body drift off into deep sleep. As I laid my head on the pillow, the Holy Spirit's still, small voice whispered softly to my heart.

"Are you ready to go?" I was almost asleep and the hour was late, but I try hard not to resist Him when He asks things of me. It's the least that I can do to thank Him for His great love.

"Yes, I am ready to go." I whispered back in the confines of my heart. *Vroooom!!!!* Instantly I was rocketing past stars with my faithful friend, Jonathan, by my side. We were zipping through space at an indescribable speed. I am not sure I had flown this fast with him before, but who knows for sure? As we ripped a tear through space, the Gate was quickly approaching. We were coming up on the Gate so fast this time that Jonathan didn't even slow down and allow it time to open. Instead he simply maintained his supersonic clip, turned us on our sides and zoomed us between the pearl bars that help fashion the Gate. We were so close to the pearl bars, I could "feel" them brush past my chest.

"Wow, that was fun!" Jonathan simply smiled back and kept up his current clip, as we raced past the beautiful golden clouds of Heaven. No chariot rides this time, just APDS (angelic person-delivery service). Jonathan banked hard and I started to see massive, towering stone or marble-like pillars coming into view. I could not see most of the structure because it was covered with clouds. Jonathan did a touch landing. My feet touched, his did not, and he was gone like a streak of light off into Heaven's golden clouds. I stood there for a few moments gathering myself. All of Heaven has His beautiful Presence, but this place felt different from anywhere I had been before. I could feel the weight of a holy hush in the air. I climbed an expansive staircase that was very wide and looked like white marble. As I reached the top, I saw a single door that was wood-like in appearance. It had an inscription above the door that I could not read. Without me asking, the Holy Spirit spoke to my heart and said one word. "Justice."

I walked through the door and I entered a room that was dripping with tension. For the first time ever in my trips to Heaven, I felt distinctly uneasy. I was standing in a courtroom at the base of the Throne. I could see part of the Throne out a long, rectangular opening on the far side of the room. I could feel the intensity of His awesome power, but I instinctively knew this was a place to stay very quiet. Light was erupting from Him, like solar flares, and His brightness was so great, I struggled to see any definition or objects in the room. As the Light erupted off of the Lord God Enthroned, it felt different than other times I had seen His Throne. There was an agitation in the air. The solar flare of Light pulsating off of Him slowed and more of the room I was standing in came into view. The room was small, and there were two podiums, facing the rectangular opening that faced the Throne. As the explosions of Light settled down some more, I could see two distinct figures standing at the two different podiums.

The figure to the right came into view first. He was hideous in appearance and I could tell he thoroughly enjoyed what he was attempting to do. I knew immediately that it was Satan. He had an insidious fanged smile, and a tar-like substance dripping from his eyes. His appearance was not of a red devil, but more of a man. I could tell he was proud of himself as he opened up a scroll and began to read from it. I could not see what was on the scroll or hear what he was saying as he read from it. I could hear his tone though, and it was dripping with accusations. When he was done reading the scroll, the figure at the other podium came into view. It was Jesus. I could only see the back of Him, from the waist up. He was dressed in a very simple robe, and I could tell His hair was dark in color.

Satan rolled up his scroll, and he looked towards Jesus, like He was awaiting an answer. Jesus spoke: "I do not know this one Father; that one is not mine." His voice was monotone and flat as He answered, yet thick, and with a depth that would reach the bottom of the deepest pit; if only it was listened to. Satan had a cunning fanged smile spread across his face, as he rolled up the scroll and handed to a black, leathery demon holding a box full of them. The demon reached into to what appeared to be a bag and pulled out another scroll. The leathery, charcoal-colored demon gleefully handed it to Satan and then shrank back into a corner and out of view. Satan, slowly and meticulously unrolled the scroll as a pride-filled expression, coursed across his twisted face. His posture appeared more pompous this time. This time I could read one word written across the top of the scroll. It said: "Believer."

Satan began to read from the scroll, with that same accusation-soaked tone. Light began to refract from The Throne again. Satan spoke louder, more Light refracted from The Throne. He spoke even louder, but he could barely stand against the Light. He tried one last time, practically shouting. Jesus spoke, and Satan immediately became silent. "Father, I know this one, this one is mine. My believer walks closely with Me and follows My Voice. My Word is written inside their heart." Jesus lifted up His right hand and I could see the place He was pierced. Light immediately exploded from The Throne and flowed through the piercing in Jesus' hand. As the Light flowed through Jesus' piercing it struck the scroll in Satan's hands and burnt it to complete ash.

Satan's face contorted with anger; he and his leathery companion quickly left the room, box in hand. Immediately, angels appeared in the room. Jesus was surrounded by them and it appeared He was giving them orders. The angel's faces were resolute and ready for battle. The Holy Spirit spoke softly to my heart. "He is commanding them to be a hedge and go protect the accused believer. This believer is filled with His Word and lives out a Kingdom-focused life." "They shake the heavens when they pray, and their faith moves the very heart of the Father Enthroned." Suddenly, I was back in my body and laying on my bed, shaken and astonished at all I had just seen.

> "So the great dragon was cast out, that serpent of old, called the Devil and Satan, who deceives the whole world; he was cast to the earth, and his angels were cast out with him. Then I heard a loud voice saying in heaven, 'Now salvation, and strength, and the kingdom of our God, and the power of His Christ have come, for the accuser of our brethren, who accused them before our God day and night, has been cast down. And they overcame him by the blood of the Lamb and by the word of their testimony, and they did not love their lives to the death.'" —Revelation 12: 9–11 NKJV

> "But He was wounded for our transgressions, He was bruised for our iniquities; The chastisement for our peace was upon Him, And by His stripes we are healed." —Isaiah 53:5 NKJV

> "Now there was a day when the sons of God came to present themselves before the Lord, and Satan also came among them. And the Lord said to Satan, 'From where do you come?' So Satan answered the Lord and said, 'From going to and fro on the earth, and from walking back and forth on it.' Then the Lord said to Satan, 'Have you considered My servant Job, that there is none like him on the earth, a blameless and upright man, one who fears God and shuns evil?' So Satan answered the Lord and said, 'Does Job fear God for

nothing? Have You not made a hedge around him, around his household, and around all that he has on every side? You have blessed the work of his hands, and his possessions have increased in the land. But now, stretch out Your hand and touch all that he has, and he will surely curse You to Your face!' And the Lord said to Satan, 'Behold, all that he has is in your power; only do not lay a hand on his person.' So Satan went out from the presence of the Lord.'"—Job 1: 6–12 NKJV

THE GATE: ETERNITY BECKONS

CHAPTER 11

THIS WAY TO THE DRESSING ROOM

"A final word: Be strong in the Lord and in His mighty power. Put on all of God's armor so that you will be able to stand firm against all strategies of the devil. You are not fighting against flesh-and-blood enemies, but against evil rulers and authorities of the unseen world, against mighty powers in this dark world, and against evil spirits in the heavenly places. Therefore, put on every piece of God's armor so you will be able to resist the enemy in the time of evil. Then after the battle you will still be standing firm. Stand your ground, putting on the belt of truth and the body armor of God's righteousness. For shoes, put on the peace that comes from the Good News so that you will be fully prepared. In addition to all of these, hold up the shield of faith to stop the fiery arrows of the devil. Put on salvation as your helmet, and take the sword of the Spirit, which is the Word of God. Pray in the Spirit at all times and on every occasion. Stay alert and be persistent in your prayers for all believers everywhere." —Ephesians 6:10–18 NLT

Many of us are familiar with this scripture, but sometimes being so familiar with something in our mind, can cause us to lose the power it brings in the spirit. It's very important that we understand that danger and be serious about the Word every time we read it. Meditate on the Word, know its power. Jesus is the Word, so reading the Word is reading about Him in all His wonder!

THE GATE: ETERNITY BECKONS

I wanted to include lots of scripture in this book to help you get jump started on that journey through the Word, and give you some great ones to memorize. Yes, I said memorize. Don't cry and hang your head; it's not too difficult to do and definitely worth your while. The more scripture you get in you, the more it will change you. Look how much it changed me from that tortured soul starting out, to an empowered man pushing His Kingdom forward. God's Word will reengineer you. You will not think the same, act the same, desire the same things, and you will lose more and more taste for this world. Your spiritual taste buds will change and you will desire to eat more and more of Heaven's delicacies.

Remember how this whole Heaven journey began with my Elias experience? After many years of private experiences in my own home, the Holy Spirit decided to do one more public one. One more public one for now; no sense in constraining Him at this point! This experience was much more subtle than the first, but still very powerful. Being seasoned in these things now, I lean much more towards anticipating His move, than being anxious about it. I trust Him and I know His ways are not my ways and His thoughts are not my thoughts. They are so much higher!

Like before, I was in a worship service and this time I was just surrendering to His Presence. The house was full and alive with activity. I was deep in worship and not seeking an experience, but the Holy Spirit fell on me and I began to shake. It's important to know that I never sought these things out and I never found my identity in them. My identity is not in the experiences, but in experiencing Him. I started to shake so hard that the Holy Spirit spoke to my heart to lay down before you fall down. I shouldn't need that instruction by now, but I still have thick places in my head and God is so gracious. I laid down, face first, and His Presence got really thick. I shook violently, and suddenly I popped out of my body! I was standing there, just like my Elias experience, looking all around, but no one looking back at me. "Well, I've been here before. Hi everyone! Never mind you don't see or hear me. Please don't step on me when I leave, I really like this shirt."

Jonathan, my tried and true friend, stood by me, smiling. He grabbed my arm, and off we went. So fun, so fast, so special. I never have and I never will take any of these experiences for granted. I love God with my whole heart, and I deeply desire to respect Him, honor Him, and see Him glorified. He is my everything. Stars blowing past, that beautiful Gate, and here we are again exploding through Heaven. Oh, the Joy! "God's people need to be equipped." Jonathan said abruptly. "They go into battle, but don't seek I AM for Wisdom and for equipping. This brings them into captivity and causes wounds they were never meant to have. Come, let me show you."

This part of Heaven looked and felt different than any place I had been before. There was an intensity in the air mixed with almost an anticipation. Anticipation of what, I did not know. We flew over a gargantuan, breathtaking meadow. The grass blew in a Wind and the flowers grew really tall. The colors of the flowers were almost neon, but that is a sad attempt at describing them. They were moving with such vibrancy. The meadow sat in an amazing valley surrounded by distant mountains. The meadow had a butte in the middle and on the top of the butte sat a tree. It was a stunning, ancient-looking tree with massive branches and a canopy that was so expansive, it seemed to hold the sky.

As we flew closer to the tree, I could see golden armor laying upon it in a very orderly fashion. Shields with shields, swords with swords, belts with belts, breastplates with breastplates, helmets with helmets, and sandals with sandals. Angels were sitting on the end of the branches almost looking bored. There was a stillness here, but the kind of stillness you feel in an old abandoned town. Angels were folding their hands, swinging their legs, whistling, pacing, and sighing. All carried a sense of tension to their actions. I could tell they wanted to be busy, but they were waiting to be released. I stared stunned and amazed, without a word coming out of my mouth.

Jonathan, in his caring way, spoke; "The saints bring many of their needs before I AM, that's what you saw at the mountain of incense. He cares for them all and hears all those requests, but the saints don't seek Him for equipping. They live their lives, only bringing their needs to I AM, but don't ask

Him to give them armor, so they can tear down darkness and take territory for His Kingdom. When Jesus came, He showed believers how to live and fight. He then specifically told the disciples not to go forth until the Helper/Comforter came. The Holy Spirit came to equip the saints, empower them, and show them how to tear down darkness. People have been deceived into believing the Holy Spirit no longer matters and He was only present for the first church. That's a lie, and many have bought into it. Because of that, saints walk without armor, and fall into various captivities. This was never I AM's plan and the saints must repent and seek Him again for the Holy Spirit. He is the Great equipper."

Suddenly, angels shot off in beams of light, carrying armor. Only a few did this, but with great power and intention. Other angels watched with excitement and anticipation.

"Jonathan, what's happening?"

"The Remnant is rising," he replied with an iron gaze.

> *"For though we walk in the flesh, we do not war according to the flesh. For the weapons of our warfare are not carnal but mighty in God for pulling down strongholds, casting down arguments and every high thing that exalts itself against the knowledge of God, bringing every thought into captivity to the obedience of Christ, and being ready to punish all disobedience when your obedience is fulfilled."* —2 Corinthians 10:4–6 NKJV

> *"And now I will send the Holy Spirit, just as my Father promised. But stay here in the city until the Holy Spirit comes and fills you with power from heaven."* —Luke 24:49 NLT

CHAPTER 12

THE GREAT PLAYGROUND

My little girl was growing and turning more beautiful every day. We had daddy/daughter dates on a regular basis, played with her doll house, had tea parties, played at the park, and so, so many laughs. She was such a beautiful gift the Lord had placed into my hands to tend and grow. The deepest thank you I could give Him was to raise her knowing Him in His fullness. I talked to her about spiritual things and read His Word to her every night. We always talk about Him just like He is in the room with us, because He is. I wanted her relationship with the Lord to feel natural and simple. I wanted her to know she can talk to Him about anything, anytime. I prayed over her eyes, ears, mind, soul and spirit, all the time.

Early on it became apparent that she had the gift of seeing in the spirit, but without the terrible torment I suffered. The curses were broken now and she was born under a line of blessing. Deuteronomy 28 is a great place to start your research on curses vs. blessings.

Going back to our story, she did see evil spirits and we called them "yucky things" when she was a toddler and then "evil things" as she grew and her understanding expanded. She saw angels too and even flowed in the gift of healing. One time I was walking down our stairs and I twisted my knee. I hurt it pretty good and was limping hard. With never showing her, she rushed over and laid her little hands on my knee. She bowed her little head and began to simply ask Jesus to bring a healing. A warm sensation like oil spread into my knee and I was totally healed. I had no pain and no limp.

My wife and I have worked hard to speak plainly about the spiritual realm and have her be free to hear from the Holy Spirit; and express what she hears in the way she understands. Everything is kept very age-appropriate, but very honest. She knows how good God really is and how evil the enemy is. Being able to distinguish the very real difference between Good and evil has brought such a protection and freedom over her life. She walks in places of freedom as a little child that it took me many years into adulthood to discover and understand.

> "One day some parents brought their children to Jesus so he could touch and bless them. But the disciples scolded the parents for bothering Him. When Jesus saw what was happening, He was angry with His disciples. He said to them, 'Let the children come to Me. Don't stop them! For the Kingdom of God belongs to those who are like these children. I tell you the truth, anyone who doesn't receive the Kingdom of God like a child will never enter it.' Then He took the children in His arms and placed His hands on their heads and blessed them." —Mark 10:13–16 NLT

Now being a father, and looking back at what I suffered through as a kid, I have come to deeply understand the importance of allowing the Holy Spirit the room to be Himself. I have learned how paramount it is to allow Him to flow freely throughout my life and my home. He won't do things on our time schedule or our convenience. He will interrupt our lives in the most beautiful of ways and lead us down the true paths of life and freedom.

If we can learn to put Him first in all things, then our lives will be orderly, blessed, abundant and free.

My little girl was so free and flowing in His power. This was a new experience for me and I went deep with the Father to learn how to partner with Him in grooming my little girl for all He had for her. I didn't want to mess this up or get in the way of His plans for her life.

One particular morning, I heard her stirring in her room and went in to get her and start our day. As I opened the door, I heard her talking to Jesus quietly on her bed. I walked in slowly and she finished up and turned to me and suddenly declared: "Hi daddy, I went to Heaven, and I really liked it." Wow! So young, so free. We sat down and had a beautiful discussion about what she experienced and saw. Everything she described to me sounded right, but then she started talking about a playground she went to and played with other kids. I questioned that part internally and wondered if this Heaven experience was a mix of imagination and real-life experiences. Little did I know, at that moment, how spot-on her full experience was. There was a depth of detail I was about to see, in a place I had yet to discover.

A few nights went by, and like so many times before, into my room Jonathan came and out of my body I jumped. It was off to Heaven again! As Jonathan walked me through the Gate, he had a chariot waiting for us. I didn't ask any questions, but instead I decided to walk right to the chariot and jump right in. I looked at the beautiful white stallion before me and said; "Hi Bill!"

The regal stallion looked over his shoulder at me and said, "Bill? I am not Bill, I am Frederick," with a smile slowly spreading across his face. Of course, you're not Bill! Ha-ha! No sense in having my small pea brain balanced now. I looked over at Jonathan and he was doubled over in laughter. "Sorry, I had to bring another horse this time just to see what you would do." Jonathan said, still holding his belly in laughter.

God's Kingdom is so fun, so good. After everyone composed themselves in the chariot we flew off into Heaven's glory. We were flying right towards the Throne when we banked hard, and started to come up on the right side of where Mighty God sat. As much as I understand distance in Heaven, you can't fly too close to the vortex that is God Almighty Himself. His raw Presence makes a Category. 5 hurricane look like someone is blowing through a straw. His Power is only matched by His beauty, which I could simply gaze at for 10,000 years without blinking.

The Gate: Eternity Beckons

This chariot ride was so different than any I had before. The closer we got to the Throne, a rainbow of colors exploded out the back of the chariot, shooting sparks everywhere. The place where we were headed to was coming into view and it was quite a party scene. It sat behind the Throne off the back of His right side. The Power emanating from the Lord over the place we were headed to, appeared to be in the shape of wings. He is the Absolute center of all life and His power is beyond immense, but the way it was emanating over this place was gentle looking, like how a mother hen would look over her chicks.

Music, dancing, and tons of laughter, pulsated from this place we were headed to. The laughter was so loud that it penetrated my spirit and I consequently broke out in laughter too. I had no idea what I was even laughing about, but I simply could not stop. I was laughing so hard, I felt as though tears could run down my face, but who knows how that works because this is my spirit man we are talking about.

With a rush of joy like you feel on a fast roller coaster, the chariot came to a stop on a beautiful piece of land mixed with clouds. As soon as we had touched down, party favors, that only Heaven could muster, erupted in all directions from our chariot. I suddenly recognized all the laughter. It was thousands of children of all different ages. As I stepped off the chariot, a massive, super-rad-looking playground was sprawling before my eyes. There were kids running and playing everywhere with such freedom and laughter. My eyes caught some different activity to the left side of the playground area. Without thinking, I stepped out of the chariot and I walked over that direction. My faithful friend Jonathan was right by my side.

I saw angels flying in, carrying little babies. The angels would fly in with the little babies and walk them into a giant room that looked just like a nursery. I looked over to Jonathan to ask a question, but he just motioned for us to continue into the building. The nursery had a mix of angels and humans tenderly caring for each of these beautiful bundles. The feeling I had in this room was a sense of responsibility. There was a mix of soberness and joy as each baby was so lovingly looked over. Jonathan gently took my elbow and motioned it was time to leave. As we exited, we walked by that super-fun-looking playground. The playground was so big that I could not see the end to it, but that incredible laughter cascaded all the way down its great expanse. It looked like a blast, and honestly, I really wanted to jump in the action, but Jonathan's body language quickly showed me we were on a mission, and staying on task was more important.

There were several different-looking buildings and what appeared to be homes all around the back side of the playground. They were innumerable. We headed specifically towards a building that distinctly had a red cross on the side of it. I saw older children being flown in by angels. Each child seemed to have some ailment or wound, but when they were brought into the building with the red cross, their ailment was healed, and they quickly ran towards the playground with overflowing joy.

Jonathan gently took my arm again and motioned it was time to go. As I made my way back to the chariot, I was having a hard time understanding what I was experiencing and what it all meant. As I stepped back into the chariot, Jonathan looked over at me and started answering the questions that were flooding through my heart. Jonathan simply said: "The babies and children you see being brought into this place are children that have wrongfully died upon the Earth. Each and every one is brought to this place to be raised, and looked after by their Heavenly Father. All their pains are healed, and they are placed in their Heavenly Father's care."

With that, we flew off and I was back in my body.

> *"How precious is your steadfast love, O God! The children of mankind take refuge in the shadow of Your wings."* —Psalms 36:7 ESV

> *"In the fear of the Lord one has strong confidence, and His children will have a refuge."* —Proverbs 14:26 ESV

> *"He who dwells in the shelter of the Most High Will abide in the shadow of the Almighty."* —Psalms 91:1 NKJV

The Gate: Eternity Beckons

"See that you do not despise one of these little ones. For I tell you that in Heaven their angels always see the face of My Father Who is in Heaven"—Matthew 18:10 ESV

CHAPTER 13

VOID TO VIBRANCY AND CONCEALED RHYTHM

I love music! Do you? Music is good for the soul, spirit, and mind and it's one part of Creation that is truly amazing. It picks us up on bad days, reminds us of loved ones, brings us together with friends, and can help heal our hearts when life brings troubles. Even plants love it. They grow better when life-giving music is played. Unfortunately, many people take this amazing gift and pervert it for their own desires. Music was created for a purpose and just like the Word says:

> *"Whatever is good and perfect comes down to us from God our Father, who created all the lights in the heavens. He never changes or casts a shifting shadow."* —James 1:17 NLT

Music was not made by mankind, it was given to us for a purpose. Because music cuts past our minds and can go straight to our emotions and spirits; it's important to bridle it correctly. How easy is it, when a good song comes on, to tap your foot, hum along, do a little dance, and not even know you are? That's the beauty of music; it rarely asks permission to go to our hearts.

Music wielded by and yielded to the Spirit of God is so beautiful, and can open Heaven's treasures over your life. Many times, visions, dreams, and even my trips to Heaven have been birthed when I was surrendered to music and yielded to His Spirit. We do have an enemy of our souls and he likes to weaponize music to bring destruction. He doesn't own it, because the Heavenly Father made it. Let that sink in for a minute; the Heavenly Father made music and gave it to us to draw us closer to Him. The enemy is the "prince of the power of the air," so as the Father sends these beautiful gifts to Earth, the enemy works hard to bring hate, anger, unforgiveness, rebellion, and many other devices to steal these gifts. He can't steal them outright, the enemy has no power over God. He gets man to agree with his perspective, and then when we do, he pounces and steals our gifts to see them perverted and be used to exalt self. I encourage you greatly to use discernment with what you allow into your soul. The Word is clear that we should guard our hearts above all things.

What about art, do you love it too? I do, and I notice it everywhere I go. I especially love animal photography, and any pieces that bring in natural elements. The right art piece can move me deeply and cause me to think. Art is beauty, and color brings such life to us. Every day I take for granted that the Father gave me the good gift of sight, designed the light to bend and reflect, so that I can see the beautiful colors that move my soul.

As I moved more and more in the things of the Spirit and saw into the invisible world, my heart broke more and more over art and music. God made and gave these amazing gifts, but we so under-utilize them to open Heaven's blessing and Power over our lives. I cannot draw, have no ability to paint, and I am not a musician, but I have a deep passion for it all. Music and art are easy gateways to the spiritual world, one gate can lead you to God's goodness and the other straight into the enemy's camp. Discernment is the key.

Flash! Brilliant light, and suddenly I was standing in Heaven. No flying this time, no angel escort, and I found myself alone staring at a cave entrance. There was a Golden Light; part mist, part fog, encompassing me as I soaked in His beautiful Peace. The Lord's Peace is everywhere in Heaven, like a warm fleece blanket wrapped around you on a cold winter day. Safe and cozy is the Way.

I did not recognize where I was in Heaven and it was different to be all alone. I figured I was sent there to go into the cave-like structure, so in I went. The entrance felt small and it was very dark. It was so dark I could not see exactly where I was going. It was not scary at all, and as I walked in, I could hear a humming, like tuning forks vibrating off the walls. I took a few more steps forward and then an angel appeared with a very messy hairdo. Though angelic in appearance and even demeanor, he appeared a bit disheveled by angel standards.

"Hi!" the angel said, with an explosive smile and joyous expression. "Welcome!"

"Where am I?" I asked.

"You are at the Void," the angel replied, still grinning ear to ear.

The angel emanated golden and white light, but the place I was in was pitch black. I felt movement, even though my eyes could not see a thing. Even in the total blackness, I could sense the room was alive, but nothing before my eyes could be seen.

"Why am I in a place where there is nothing?" I asked.

"Nothing!" the angel roared, with a gleeful shout. Suddenly the angel fell down laughing and laughing, holding his belly. I don't know how long I stood there, but he belly-laughed so hard and long at my question, that I borderline felt awkward. "Everything was created from nothing!" the angel said as he fell down in complete laughter again. Okay, now this is awkward. Haha! After a while, the angel stood up and looked me right in the eyes with great intensity. "I AM specializes in creating life out of what appears to be nothing. Where you are standing is the origin of color and expression." Out of the darkness and void, I started to feel a vibration. It started at my feet, then suddenly permeated my whole being. I tried standing still, but I was being moved by the whole pulsating sensation.

Boom!!! Green color shot out in a stream of light before my eyes! Boom!!! Now blue, then yellow, red, purple, exploded before my eyes. It sounded like a reverberating electric guitar strum, with a deep resonant bass vibration. That is the best way I can describe the sound of color coming to life. It excites you and then moves you down to your core, while captivating your soul. As color continued to burst in front of me, I could hear laughter from all around that would make Earth's best 5.1 surround-sound systems sound like a sad whimper. The laughter was alive and appeared like liquid gold. This liquid gold began to mix with various colors, and the combinations were erupting all over the cave.

"This is the essence of expression, the very origin of the gift itself," the angel said. Suddenly, that golden light, part mist, part fog, appeared all around me. The Holy Spirit whispered to my heart that He had more to show me and that it was time to exit this place.

I slowly walked towards the direction I came from; all the while feeling the laughter mixed with color coursing through my soul. What a fun place indeed! As I fully exited, I found myself standing amongst, and on, clouds, yet my feet felt like they were on solid ground.

I looked straight ahead and could see a humble-looking man sitting on a simple wooden chair. His face was kind and his beard was very long. His eyes were intensely direct and yet very inviting. Behind him was a massive gorge that was completely impassable. Beyond the gorge I could see an object that appeared to be pulsating, but I had no idea what it was. The "man" stood and motioned me to come closer. As I approached him, he vanished and evaporated into the clouds. The clouds began to part and as they did, massive stone tablets appeared that had the entire book of Proverbs written on them.

Suddenly a voice began to speak and I heard; "I AM Wisdom and too many believers ignore My voice and give Me no place. Their pride is their downfall and they are taken captive because they do not want to know Me. I challenge their thinking and ask for self-sacrifice. I ask that they lay down their own lives and desires for My Glory, not their own. They believe their own talents and knowledge are the way to success, but that folly leads to their destruction. If they would dine with Me, listen to My voice, they would find Life and that Life has Eternal rewards. I AM their strong tower, but they run from Wisdom and believe in their hearts that Wisdom and knowledge are the same thing. They are not! Wisdom and Understanding are Life itself. They believe because they have knowledge, they may use the knowledge of the gifts I give to benefit themselves. This is not the Way or the Truth. Believers must lay their gifts and talents at My feet. They must desire and earnestly seek Wisdom on how to use them; then My Presence and Power can transform lives through them."

I cannot express the emotions I felt in that moment. I had no words, only a contriteness within me and a desire to once again lay my life down.

My gaze moved from the tablets back towards the gorge. Clouds moved across the great gorge and in the midst of them a solid, very wide, rock bridge appeared.

Wisdom spoke again. "If My people will lay down all they think is right in their own eyes, and seek My voice, then solid paths will be made before them that lead to Life and Life more abundantly."

I knew I was to walk across the bridge, and so I went towards it. As I crossed over the bridge, my heart was in a deep place of contriteness and brokenness. I wanted more of Him and I wanted to go deeper with Him in every way. As I exited the bridge, the object that was once far away, was now right in front of me. Musical notes emanated from it and the sound was like nothing I have ever heard on Earth. The sound was as if Life Itself was singing. I could hear singing in one accord, so beautiful, it had a rhythm that felt like water to the soul. So still, so pure, so powerful. What was the object before me, you ask? It was a giant, golden, beating Heart.

Wisdom spoke again, "You are standing at the very origin of song and music. If my people would only hear My voice, and partner with Me, there are many creative expressions and beautiful stories I would love to tell through their lives."

"In the beginning God created the heavens and the earth. Now the earth was formless and void, and darkness was over the surface of

the deep. And the Spirit of God was hovering over the surface of the waters." —Genesis 1:1–2 NKJV

"O Lord, what a variety of things you have made! In Wisdom you have made them all. The earth is full of your creatures." —Psalms 104:24 NLT

"When You give them Your breath, life is created, and You renew the face of the earth. May the glory of the Lord continue forever! The Lord takes pleasure in all He has made! The earth trembles at His glance; the mountains smoke at His touch. I will sing to the Lord as long as I live. I will praise my God to my last breath! May all my thoughts be pleasing to Him, for I rejoice in the Lord." —Psalms 104:30–34 NLT

"Speaking to yourselves in psalms and hymns and spiritual songs, singing and making melody in your heart to the Lord; Giving thanks always for all things unto God and the Father in the name of our Lord Jesus Christ." —Ephesians 5:19–20 NKJV

"Praise the Lord! Praise God in His sanctuary; Praise Him in His mighty firmament! Praise Him for His mighty acts; Praise Him according to His excellent greatness! Praise Him with the sound of the trumpet; Praise Him with the lute and harp! Praise Him with the timbrel and dance; Praise Him with stringed instruments and flutes! Praise Him with loud cymbals; Praise Him with clashing cymbals! Let everything that has breath praise the Lord. Praise the Lord!" —Psalms 150:1–6 NKJV

". . .but to those who are called, both Jews and Greeks, Christ the power of God and the wisdom of God. Because the foolishness of God is wiser than men, and the weakness of God is stronger than men." —1 Corinthians 1:24–25 ESV

"Get wisdom! Get understanding! Do not forget, nor turn away from the words of my mouth. Do not forsake her, and she will pre-

serve you; Love her, and she will keep you. Wisdom is the principal thing; Therefore get wisdom. And in all your getting, get understanding. Exalt her, and she will promote you; She will bring you honor, when you embrace her." —Proverbs 4:5–8 NKJV

"The fear of the Lord is the beginning of wisdom, And the knowledge of the Holy One is understanding. Wisdom will multiply your days and add years to your life. If you become wise, you will be the one to benefit. If you scorn wisdom, you will be the one to suffer." —Proverbs 9:10–12 NKJV

THE GATE: ETERNITY BECKONS

CHAPTER 14

BANK ACCOUNT, BOOM!

You have arrived! You made it to your personal launch pad. Are you ready? Have you been soaking in this adventure and memorizing the scriptures? If not, go back and read them again, and tell a friend. I'm serious. . . go!

Did you do it? Good, it's time to move forward, it's time to take territory, and it's time for you to discover your purpose and call. He loves you, He made you, He calls out to you, and He wants you with Him forever. Don't hesitate to answer His call. He doesn't leave voicemails, so make sure you answer when you hear His voice ringing in your heart.

Destiny is a word that many of us wrestle with. It's such a deep word, but hard to catch. An ache inside of us that we all pursue, but so few find it. He has designed each of us uniquely, to reflect Him like no one else can. You are made in His image and He desires to show off Who He is through you. He broke the mold when He made you and you will never be repeated. You are a gem that is handcrafted, a royal priesthood, and a joint heir. Never forget that. You have a purpose and design; come, let's discover it.

The Holy Spirit led me to share a story that can help you put movement to all you have learned. Grab your armor, fight the Good fight, and let's take down darkness together.

THE GATE: ETERNITY BECKONS

I've wrestled with the word *destiny;* you have wrestled with the word *destiny*. Let's discover His answer together, shall we?

It was a warm afternoon and I had just gotten back to my house from walking my dog. I made a sandwich, and got a cold drink. As I sat down on my couch, Jonathan walked through the front door.

"You didn't knock."

"Well, if I did, you would not hear me, and I thought a nice surprise was in order today." Jonathan replied, a smile across his face.

I sat my triple-decker sandwich down, stacked with yumminess, because I knew now was not a time to eat. I thought maybe I was just going to have a conversation with Jonathan about something, but nope, today a flight was scheduled on my behalf. As the Holy Spirit began to fall into the room, I surrendered to His incredible peace. He is so good.

My mind drifted back to my sandwich, if only for a moment. I did have my priorities in order, but that sandwich took some serious time to craft. Okay, enough of that, moving on from my foodie problem now.

I let His Presence wash over me and just like that, no shaking, I just stepped out of my body and next to Jonathan. Jonathan grabbed me by the arm, and we were off to the races, through the roof, over the Earth, zooming past stars! There it was, the Gate, fashioned out of solid pearl. No matter how many times I've seen it, it feels like the first time, always stunning, always sobering, as it points straight to John 14:6 NKJV, Jesus answered, "I am the Way, the Truth, and the Life. No one comes to the Father except through Me."

As I walked through the Gate, I was immediately approached by an angel in a business suit.

"We have an appointment."

"An appointment?"

"Yes, it's time for you to get an answer for an issue that has long been unsettled in your heart."

You see, destiny always nagged me and yet eluded me. I never really understood how to discover it. I look to man too often to give me answers that all along the Father wanted to give.

As I entered deeper into Heaven, the magnitude overtook me. With somewhere so big, where do I look? I don't want to miss anything! Colors outside of our world, yet totally recognizable, music without beat, yet you feel the rhythm, the air you breath is not oxygen, but the perfect blend of Love, Peace, and Light. You don't actually breathe it in, it flows in you and through you, saturating every part of you.

We stopped at a massive, pure-gold building. Combine all the fanciest, swankiest, banks you have ever seen, in all the Earth, and you are just starting to get a glimpse of this place. I stumbled and stammered a bit as I walked through the front door, amazed at how everything was pure gold. It was the purest gold my eyes had ever seen. I walked up to an angel at a front desk and asked, "What is this place?"

"This is one of the storage houses for the Bride's destiny."

"One?"

"Yes, there are many storage houses in Heaven."

The angel motioned for me to take a look. As my gaze pathetically tried to take in the vastness, I knew there was no way I could. Imagine, 1000 times the size of the Grand Canyon, just to look down one hall. Yes, that was the size! No details, not one, gets past the Eternal gaze of the Father.

> *"But you, when you pray, go into your room, and when you have shut the door, pray to your Father who is in the secret place; and your Father who sees in secret will reward you openly. And when you pray, do not use vain repetitions as the heathen do. For they think that they will be heard for their many words. Therefore do*

not be like them. For your Father knows the things you have need of before you ask Him." —Matthew 6:6–8 NKJV

I decided at that point to try and focus more on the small details, instead of the vastness. I soon realized, there where millions upon millions of security boxes, each individually marked with specific wording on them. Imagine the types of safe-deposit boxes you see in a bank vault. The kind that are long and metal, and all individually marked. These were the same way, except they were all pure gold and each one had a different word on it, in a language I did not recognize. As I gazed at all the boxes, another angel motioned for me to come into a room.

I entered the room, and I noticed he had one of the boxes setting on a table of pure gold, just like the whole building. He had a key to unlock it, and on the box was written a very long name that started with the letters EROC.

"What is this box and what does the writing mean?"

"This box contains your individual destiny, the writing is your Heavenly name. Your Heavenly name gets inscribed on everything the Father prepares for you."

"What does the name mean?"

"Founded on the Rock, but that is only the first part."

"Would you like to see inside?"

"Yes, please!!!!!" Just then, the angel opened the box. . .

Your destiny awaits. . .

"Whatever is good and perfect comes down to us from God our Father, who created all the lights in the heavens. He never changes or casts a shifting shadow. "—James 1:17 NLT

"His purpose was that now, through the church, the manifold wisdom of God should be made known to the rulers and authorities in

the heavenly realms, according to the eternal purpose that He accomplished in Christ Jesus our Lord. In Him and through faith in Him we may enter God's presence with boldness and confidence."
—Ephesians 3:10–12 ESV

"For people swear by something greater than themselves, and in all their disputes an oath is final for confirmation. So when God desired to show more convincingly to the heirs of the promise the unchangeable character of His purpose, He guaranteed it with an oath, so that by two unchangeable things, in which it is impossible for God to lie, we who have fled for refuge might have strong encouragement to hold fast to the hope set before us." —Hebrews 6:16–18 NLT

THE GATE: ETERNITY BECKONS

CHAPTER 15

THE GREAT WATCHMAN

Our final on-ramp is here. I sure hope you have enjoyed the journey as much as I've enjoyed telling it! We have gone so many places together and discovered the smallest glimpse of how vast and deep He and His Kingdom are.

This particular trip to Heaven actually caught me off guard. I had just finished a fun-filled day with my little girl. We played with her doll house, ran through the house pretending to be superheroes, played outside, and finished the day watching one of her favorite shows together. It's hard to say who was more worn out at the end of the day. I'll call it even, because I decided to go to bed shortly after I laid her down for the night.

My mind was tired and honestly, I was not focused on anything Heavenly. I was just thinking about all the fun I had that day with my cute little girl. Suddenly, Jonathan appeared in my room, standing next to my bed. It actually startled me!

"I didn't pack a suitcase."

"That's okay, I'll bring you back soon and will make sure you don't get your clothes dirty."

Whooshh! An explosion of light and power and once again I was off to Heaven.

The Gate: Eternity Beckons

As we arrived at the Gate, I asked Jonathan where we were going this time. "Not very deep in this time, just going to take you to the very outskirts. You will understand when you get there," Jonathan said. He held my arm tightly as we banked hard right. Who knows how fast we were going, but I certainly felt the rush of speed.

I saw a long rectangular structure coming into view. It was covered in clouds of gold and mist, but on solid ground. As we descended, I could see thousands and thousands of stalls in one great stable. On earth, I have had the opportunity to be in some truly beautiful houses. Homes well beyond 10,000 square feet, overlooking some of the most beautiful natural scenery human eyes could conceive. Homes that would move your soul from their sheer architectural design or the amazing landscaping. I have been in homes on earth with some of the rarest art pieces the world has to offer, but none of those homes would touch the beauty of just one of the stalls I was now looking at in Heaven.

"Stop being wrapped up with the things of a fallen world." Jonathan said. "That's what I AM wants His people to know." Jonathan continued. "He wants His people to advance His Kingdom and use the tools that He paid for on the Cross. He wants to demonstrate His Greatness through His people, but they are too wrapped up with the cares of that fallen world." His eyes were balls of fire as he spoke. I only listened.

I stood there taking in the magnitude of where I was standing. I could hear the movement of mighty horses, I could feel they were restless and ready to run. I wondered for a minute if Bill was in one of the stalls, but considering I was looking at a stable the size of a city, I am not sure how I would find him if he were.

I was still a good distance from the main artery of the stalls, and I started to walk that direction to get a closer look. Suddenly, Jonathan gently grabbed my arm and said "no." He pointed ahead to what looked like the very edge of where we were standing. At the edge I could see a figure standing, but the light around was so intense, it was nearly impossible to make out the figure's form.

"Go now, someone is waiting for you and wants to talk with you." Jonathan said.

I looked ahead at the figure off in the distance, then back at Jonathan. I am not sure if you can have butterflies in your stomach in Heaven, but that is the best way I can describe my feelings. Totally at peace, but this was so different than all my other experiences; I felt nervous. Jonathan motioned that I should go forward, so off I went. I passed by row after row after row after row of stalls. I could feel the stirring of this place, pent-up action, waiting to explode.

I made my way closer to the figure, and I suddenly realized Who I was looking at. I only saw His back at first. He had a multicolored robe that moved as though a Wind was blowing in that place. His hair was shoulder length, and white as snow and yet the very essence of light itself. I could see He had a crown on His head and as I looked towards His feet they were brass-like, with fire and power emitting from them. I was frozen still, somewhere between falling on my face and completely paralyzed.

The color cascading from Him and dancing about where nothing my eyes have ever seen before. His brilliance was indescribable. His back was still towards me, with His right shoulder slightly turned back. He put out His right hand, and I saw the nail scar. He motioned with His hand for me to come to Him, and somehow strength entered my legs enough to walk. I stood next to Jesus and caught the first glimpse of His beautiful face. He IS the Way, the Truth, the Life and all will bow before Him, no questions asked. He IS. His face was kind and His gaze was straight forward.

I knew in the Spirit it was okay to be there and to just wait. He motioned for me to come forward and look in the direction He was looking. As I came even with Him, the power and intensity of His face was more than I could bear. I almost broke right there, right then, and He had not even looked my way. I felt myself shaking and just to be by Him answered every question a person could ever muster, without a word being spoken. I took my eyes from Him and looked in the direction He had motioned.

THE GATE: ETERNITY BECKONS

It was the Earth, suspended there, like a beautiful blue marble. I looked back at Him and He was still gazing upon it. Next to Him stood the most regal, powerful, majestic, and flat-out intimidating white stallion I have ever seen. Its mane blew in the same Wind that was all around Jesus. Jesus had His hand on the stallion, slightly touching its bare back. Jesus' gaze was flint-like, His jaw strong and fixed and His eyes were a mix of a thousand galaxies and burning fire. The focus on what He had before Him was unflinching.

I could only look at Him for a few seconds, before His awesome presence overwhelmed me. I fell to my face with no words, just totally bowed down. All strength left my being. I was undone in His presence. Suddenly, I heard His voice in my heart speaking to me to arise. Strength entered my legs and I stood once again. He slowly turned and looked at me, and His eyes changed to the deepest blue I've ever seen. Such Love, such Compassion, such Peace, such Absoluteness.

He spoke softly, "My people do not believe I am coming back. Tell them I am coming soon." His gaze turned away from me, back towards the Earth, and then suddenly I was back in my room on Earth.

> *"And behold, I am coming quickly, and My reward is with Me, to give to every one according to his work. I am the Alpha and the Omega, the Beginning and the End, the First and the Last."*
> —Revelation 22:12–13 NKJV

53366493R00066

Made in the USA
Lexington, KY
30 September 2019